UNITED STATES
OF
FEAR

UNITED STATES
OF
FEAR

HOW AMERICA FELL VICTIM
TO A MASS DELUSIONAL PSYCHOSIS

Mark McDonald M.D.

BOMBARDIER
BOOKS

PUBLISHED BY BOMBARDIER BOOKS
An Imprint of Post Hill Press
ISBN: 978-1-63758-319-7
ISBN (eBook): 978-1-63758-320-3

Cover Design by Tiffani Shea

Post Hill Press
New York • Nashville
posthillpress.com

Published in the United States of America

Contents

The Other Pandemic: The Making of a Mass Delusional Psychosis

I N THE SUMMER of 2020, the mother of a fifteen-year-old boy with ADHD declined to bring him to my office for his three-month medication follow-up visit. "We haven't been going out much recently," she explained. The boy had been my patient for eight years, and I had seen him regularly every ninety days throughout that entire period. He came from a rather typical, upper-middle-class West Los Angeles family with two parents. He was an only child. He was a good student and quite sociable, with no significant problems other than his ADHD, which had been well-managed for many years. His mother had always appeared anxious and somewhat controlling. I found his father to be warm, easygoing, and calm if a bit passive and unassertive. All three were likable people who had never challenged any of my clinical recommendations.

After insisting that an in-person visit would be necessary for optimal care, I suggested she drop him off at

the building instead. He was old enough to come up-
stairs by himself. This launched her into a hysterical rant
about the dangers of her son walking through a public
building and the health risk he would assume, not to
mention the possibility of the family contracting a terrifying, highly contagious disease.

Despite evidence to the contrary—that children are
essentially immune to the Chinese Wuhan virus and even
act as barriers to its spread—she insisted that I was unin-
formed, unreasonable, and cruel for demanding that her
son come to my office in person to discuss his medica-
tions. A day later, I received another email, this one from
her husband, apologizing on behalf of his wife, thanking
me for helping care for their son all these years, but announcing that they would be seeking a new psychiatrist.

Reading between the lines, I interpreted his message to be, "My wife is hysterical, and there is nothing
I can do about it. To preserve our marriage, I must go
along with her demand to switch doctors to someone
who will treat him over Zoom and keep him under house
arrest until she regains her senses."

From these brief exchanges, it was clear to me that
a previously anxious woman had deteriorated into a delusional state, and that her husband could not find the
courage to manage her in any helpful way, so he chose
to collude with her pathology rather than take charge of
his own family.

I am a psychiatrist—a medical doctor. I have evalu-
ated and treated both children and adults for psychiatric
illness for over ten years, in a variety of settings that have
included in-patient hospitals, residential treatment programs, and jails. For the past eight years, my focus has
been outpatient care, mainly through my solo clinical

practice in Los Angeles. This has allowed me to offer medication treatment and talk therapy, or a combination of both. Treating children has been of particular interest to me, which is why I earned a second board certification in child and adolescent psychiatry.

I have seen thousands of patients. Several hundred fill my current practice. Most have been with me for at least two years, and many for five years or more. I always treat my patients with honesty and respect, but I do challenge them, make every effort not to collude with their pathology, and set the expectation that they do the work necessary to get better. My treatment philosophy is that acknowledging truth and reality is essential for a patient to make real progress. This acknowledgement often makes the patient uncomfortable and can even cause real suffering. But there is no shortcut to growth, and self-deception only serves as an obstacle to psychological wellness.

Fear is not new to me. I treat many children and adults who are, at some level, afraid. They express their fear through anxiety, phobias, obsessions and compulsions, and even psychosis. Fear is not a bad thing, in and of itself. Like pain, fear serves to protect us from injury. Without it, human beings would be prone to taking unnecessary risks and all wind up dead before even reproducing. Fearless humans are quickly removed from the gene pool through natural selection.

But fear can also be harmful when it arrives at the wrong time, for the wrong reason, or beyond the length of time that it is needed. We all know someone who suffers from chronic or neuropathic pain, conditions that bring such a degree of suffering to life that existence itself often becomes intolerable. Daily life cannot be enjoyed due to the constant distraction of physical pain.

Far from being protective, this sort of pain condition is nothing short of extended torture.

On an emotional level, pathologic fear produces the same result—it paralyzes one from engaging with life. When fear no longer protects from harm but simply inhibits one from living fully, it ceases to be helpful. When fear becomes the primary driver of decision-making, the quality of our decisions begins to suffer.

Although every one of us lives with a degree of fear, for some people, the fear becomes so great, so impairing, so insufferable, that they come to me looking for a solution. Whether it's insomnia, panic attacks, obsessions and compulsions, or melancholic depression, that solution often involves medication, some form of talk therapy, or both.

Pathological fear not only harms the individual—it also harms families, communities, and society at large. A child who cannot sleep through the night due to regular nightmares will prevent his parents from sleeping. An overly cautious driver on the freeway will provoke accidents that harm and possibly kill people nearby.

The effects magnify when groups of people become caught up in fear. One well-known consequence: To prevent the possibility of even minor injury, playground equipment in many schools and parks has been removed, depriving children of the opportunity to grow and develop through play.

In the extreme, when fear spreads throughout an entire society, the effect is paralyzing. Decision-making becomes irrational and reactive. The sensationalizing of outlier events and the pursuit of safety supplants sound public policy. Media begin covering the "fear story" and serving it to their audience on a regular basis. Fear-driven official pronouncements evoke more fear among the citizenry, who demand more protection from politicians. A vicious cycle ensues. Mass hysteria develops, and people lose their capacity to think and act rationally.

This becomes dangerous, similar to the way a mob functions—acting on pure groupthink and raw emotion. It's a form of developmental regression that hobbles society. Unfortunately, there is no cure for fear on a societal level. The only way to address it is individually, one patient at a time.

Although psychiatric illness is to a large degree biologically driven by genetics, diet, and exercise, environment plays a significant role in generating trends. Children and adolescents, for example, suffer more anxiety today than when I began my career. Although there are multiple reasons for this, the most important one, from my perspective as a clinician, is the rise of social media. Regardless of the country studied, the adolescent population shows a predisposition to internet and cell phone addiction, which strongly correlates with sleep deficit, anxiety, stress, and depression. Since I began working predominantly with young people in 2010, I have seen a steady, gradual worsening of emotional functioning—particularly in elementary-school-age patients—as cell phone use has expanded. It's not uncommon now for fourth- and fifth-graders to carry their own phones with them. Many pull them out of their pockets reflexively the moment they sit down in my office, burying their faces in the little screen.

Their parents often explain to me how this is the way they communicate with their friends—by sending text messages and pictures. Watching video after video allows them to tune out their immediate environment. Most children find it intolerable to be told to put their phone away for any extended period, as disconnecting from the online world activates a cascade of anxiety. It should come as no surprise, then, that anxiety is now the most common psychiatric diagnosis in the youth population.

When the pandemic arrived in 2020, a new expression of fear emerged. Across the full patient spectrum, complaints of worry, insomnia, and drug cravings increased. Patients of mine who had been stable for months or years suddenly required medication dose changes. Former patients returned for therapy because they were struggling to cope. New patients nearly universally cited anxiety as their reason for seeking help.

Although many could not identify the source of their anxiety, most admitted feeling unsafe. "I'm having nightmares for the first time." "I'm so preoccupied that I haven't had sex in six weeks." "I hate to admit it, but the only thing I look forward to now is a stiff drink at the end of the day." Parents of my child patients started reporting new-onset bedwetting, social isolation, explosive rage, and acts of violence toward siblings.

By summer, the wave of fear that had swept my Los Angeles practice appeared to be spreading throughout the city and indeed across the country. In April 2020, the director of the Didi Hirsch Suicide Prevention Center announced the hotline had received 1,800 calls in March compared to only twenty in February. Businesses began limiting hours or closing entirely. Schools shut their doors. Car traffic dwindled and streets emptied of pedestrians. If you were fortunate enough to even come across another human being walking outside, that stranger would most likely cross the street.

Los Angeles announced a de facto ban on people leaving their homes, although this mandate was largely ignored due to its sheer impracticality. Instead, local bureaucrats settled for universal outdoor mask mandates, calling city police officers to ticket offenders who dared to breathe freely while driving in their cars with the windows open. One day a contractor working on my house complained to me that, on his way over, he had been stopped by Beverly Hills police for driving while maskless. "If your windows are open, you have to wear a mask," he was told. Fortunately, he was let go with a warning. I noticed in my regular walks around the neighborhood that few people would greet or even acknowledge me. Many would avoid me entirely by abandoning the sidewalk in preference for using the street for their afternoon strolls. I never wore a mask outdoors, and I am certain this terrified them.

At times the hyperbolic crackdown on individuals going about their day-to-day lives revealed itself in farcical yet poignant news highlights, such as local police arresting a man for paddle-boarding alone in the Pacific Ocean. This story made national headlines for its manifest absurdity.

Most surprising, though, was the absence of any significant opposition to these fear-driven government policies. As hundreds, even thousands, of Los Angelenos rioted in the streets on behalf of "racial justice," the same people appeared to be in total agreement with the need to severely curtail personal liberties in order to keep everyone safe from infection.

Rather than explain the scientific basis for their decisions, politicians and unelected bureaucrats simply repeated empty slogans such as "Better safe than sorry" and "We're all in this together." In April 2020, New York Governor Andrew Cuomo famously said, in defending his statewide lockdown policy, "If it saves just one life, I'll be happy."

This absurd fallacy became the basis for many destructive policies to come, most of which accomplished little or nothing and, in fact, actually cost many American lives. In 2020, nearly 40,000 Americans died in traffic accidents according to a National Highway Traffic Safety Administration report. Nearly all those lives could have been saved had we reduced the speed limit to fifteen miles per hour. Of course, we would never do that because it would incapacitate the country. Long-distance travel would end, commute times would exceed hours worked in many cases, and overall productivity would decline to a level that would no longer sustain our current standard of living. In other words, there would be a cost. But the question of cost never came up when government officials chose to impose lockdowns, announcing with great conviction but not a shred of evidence that countless lives would be saved.

I was deeply puzzled and alarmed by what I was seeing. A viral pandemic had begun, but I could see no reason why that should have led to a draconian citywide lockdown. Nor could I explain how it had caused such a rapid, profound, and nearly universal deterioration in mental health. Americans had suffered viral pandemics before—Spanish flu, SARS, MERS, and H1N1. Some of these pandemics developed into true health emergencies, unlike the most recent arrival that reliable data showed to be essentially benign for all but a fraction of the population.

It was clear as early as March that most deaths in the US were occurring in specific subgroups, mainly those people sixty-five years of age and older (more than 80 percent of all deaths) and those living in nursing homes (only one percent of the US population). If you were young and healthy—or just healthy—your risk of death from the Wuhan virus was likely no greater than that of dying in a car crash. Try as I might, I could find no objective rationale for any of the government measures or a reasonable explanation for the explosion in mental illness.

Meanwhile, I began to see people being shut down for trying to discuss and debate basic policy issues affecting the prevention and treatment of the disease or its negative social effects. This suffocation of any public conversation critical of government policy or recommendations made me suspicious of the scientific basis for the direction our country was being led. If an evidence-based cost analysis had really been made, shouldn't the evidence be available for inspection?

I first decided to enter the public sphere in my professional capacity by co-writing an opinion piece for the LA Daily News published on April 18, 2020. I had never done this before, but a colleague specializing in ophthalmology invited me to join him in questioning the basis of Los Angeles Mayor Eric Garcetti's "Safer at Home" order. I suggested that keeping people locked down in their homes was contributing to the psychological breakdown I saw throughout the city. I cited the previous month's explosion in calls to Didi Hirsch as evidence.

I knew I was taking a risk. Many L.A. residents supported the lockdown, as they were promised that it would save lives. They were told it was necessary to get us through a once-in-a-lifetime viral pandemic. Yet I could find no evidence to support this claim. The mayor's order was later followed at the federal level with the now-infamous "fifteen days to flatten the curve" pronouncement aimed at keeping the nation's hospitals from becoming overwhelmed. The policy I had challenged at the local level had now gone national.

Fortunately, our article did not provoke any attacks against me or cause me to lose patients. In fact, it appeared to go largely unnoticed, as I received no responses from any readers. It did bring me to the attention of an emergency room physician, though, who was suffering from considerable pushback from her employer for her advocacy of aggressive early outpatient treatment for symptomatic viral pandemic patients.

Dr. Simone Gold, who went on to found America's Frontline Doctors, called me to ask if I would be interested in participating in a doctors' summit to bring attention to government and institutional mismanagement of the pandemic. Coincidentally, I heard Dr. Gold a week earlier on AM radio while driving to work. Dennis Prager, a local talk show host with a daily broadcast heard throughout the country, had invited her on his show to discuss her personal experience as an ER physician at a hospital just north of Los Angeles. "For the first time," she said, "my medical decision-making was being challenged and overruled by my colleagues."

Citing scientific evidence of benefit in reducing symptoms of infection from the Wuhan virus, she had begun treating her patients with hydroxychloroquine, a medication that had been safely used in the US for decades to treat lupus and rheumatoid arthritis. Everything she said sounded so reasonable and uncontroversial that I was shocked to hear she was being treated so harshly with no justification. At the time, I thought to myself, "Something new and disturbing is happening." I knew she was on to something, perhaps something really big. So it didn't take me long to agree to participate in the event she was organizing.

Before the first Frontline Doctors Summit at the end of July, I had plenty of time to observe the wrong direction the country was heading in. The school year had ended abruptly in mid-March, all "nonessential" businesses had been forcibly closed by local government, and many cities had instituted outdoor mask mandates. Most concerning to me as a child and adolescent psychiatrist was the psychological harm being done by these poorly considered decisions. Many parents were refusing to bring their children to see me, frightened they or their children would catch a fatal disease simply by coming to my office.

One told me his eight-year-old son had put his fist through a plate-glass window at home, unable to tolerate being confined to a two-room apartment twenty-four hours a day for months on end. Another patient began wetting the bed again. Yet another attacked her brother with a kitchen knife. Later that summer, in speaking with colleagues around the country at conferences and sharing clinical experiences with them through group email, I discovered that this was happening everywhere. My inbox would eventually be flooded with pleas from desperate parents, begging me for advice on what to do with their emotionally distraught children. Most mainstream news sources chose not to report this side of the lockdown story, as it exposed a cost that few wanted to acknowledge.

I knew that closing schools was a terrible decision. It made no medical sense—Sweden had kept its schools open with no increase in disease—yet American school boards foolishly believed it was better for children to sit at home all day, alone, confined to their rooms, living through their computers and cell phones. When I was invited in June by the Orange County Board of Education to speak on an expert panel on re-opening the schools, I immediately agreed.

The meeting was packed. Parents unable to get in stood outside in the parking lot, jockeying for a spot to listen through the open door. One of several experts called to speak on behalf of school re-opening, I sat through several hours of speeches, question and answer, debate, and remote Zoom call-in statements. I had no prepared remarks.

When I was at last invited to deliver a closing statement, I spoke briefly, but from the heart. "Why are we even having this meeting tonight? We're meeting because we adults are afraid." I went on to say, "We must agree to make decisions in the best interest of the children. If we do not—if, paralyzed by fear, we continue to act purely out of self-interest—we will ensure an entire generation of traumatized young people, consigned to perpetual adolescence and residency in their parents' garages, unable to move through life with independence, courage, and confidence. They deserve better—we owe it to them as parents." Those words were later reproduced in the *Wall Street Journal*'s Notable & Quotable column.

One month later, I found myself standing alongside Dr. Gold and a dozen other physicians on the steps of the Supreme Court in Washington, D.C., speaking to a live audience of millions on the viral pandemic and the growing catastrophe of the government response to it. In my remarks, I focused on the closure of America's schools, calling it "the greatest mistake in the government response to the pandemic." I went on to explain how America was indeed suffering from a pandemic, but not a medical one. Instead, it was a pandemic of fear. This fear pandemic was taking a far greater toll on our lives than any virus ever could. And I stated that it was up to all of us to acknowledge our fear and act in spite of it.

This Breitbart live internet broadcast reached over two million people in under an hour and nearly fifteen million more in the hours following. None of us had expected such an overwhelming reception. What came next, though, was even more shocking: Later that night, the original recording and all re-posts were taken down by Facebook, YouTube, and Twitter. As this was occurring, President Trump and his son tweeted links to our talk. The tweets were taken down, and Don Jr.'s account was suspended.

America's Frontline Doctors had clearly hit a nerve. We had told the truth about the pandemic and the failure of our government to properly respond to it. Our punishment was universal censorship. Everything we had said was factual, medically sound, and backed up by empirical evidence, but we had challenged the pandemic narrative, and that was not allowed.

I returned to Los Angeles with first-hand experience of the seriousness of the crisis—not a medical crisis, but a crisis of misinformation, censorship, and government overreach. From the exposure I had received in Washington, D.C., calls started coming in from live radio shows and podcasters. For several weeks, I was scheduled for an interview nearly every workday. The topic was always the same: fear and the push to trade freedom for the promise of safety. Very few physicians were addressing the topic of harm being done to children from this twisted Faustian bargain. Although controversial, it was impossible to deny that Americans were paying a steep price to treat their anxiety. For the first time in my life, I saw the removal of civil liberties occurring under the guise of safety. And fear was fueling it.

But Americans were not only suffering from fear. A psychotic thought process had developed, where irrationality was driving both individual and group behavior. I noticed it with my patients and the public. It's one thing to reflexively respond to a new threat—the potential of human extinction by way of a virus—by panicking and withdrawing from society, like a frightened animal that runs under the house on July 4th after the fireworks begin. That was the basis for the "fifteen days to slow the spread" policy announcement by the government. By summer, though, we were long past that point. Hospitals were not overwhelmed, healthy people were not dying in large numbers, and anyone who did receive early treatment invariably survived.

This was self-evident, yet a large segment of society continued to voluntarily sequester at home, wear masks outdoors, and perform other superstitious and scientifically baseless rituals like wiping down Amazon deliveries with bleach. I knew one man whose wife insisted on taking off her clothes whenever she returned home and throwing them in the dryer for "sterilization." That is insanity. Previously normal-appearing individuals had clearly lost their minds. Worse, these behaviors were not limited to a handful of people. I read reports of extreme changes in thoughts and actions from all over the country, primarily from large urban centers. Much of the nation had disconnected from basic reality. I began to call this condition a "mass delusional psychosis."

Adopting a worldview that rejects and attacks reality is psychotic. Although we most often see it in individuals—cult leaders, homeless drug addicts, celebrity stalkers—psychotic illness can also affect groups of people and, indeed, whole societies. This can happen when everyone becomes hyperfocused on one issue, when fear becomes the predominant emotion, and rational faculties become paralyzed en masse. That is exactly what happened to Americans in 2020.

Many people believe psychosis involves seeing or hearing things that aren't there. That is a perceptual disturbance common with schizophrenics. It shows up frequently in movie characters who are described as psychotic. It's easy to distinguish a psychotic person from a non-psychotic person in this way because, in general, we can all agree on what we see and hear—those aspects of our experience are not open to broad interpretation. Calling someone psychotic is also widely considered derogatory, as the term is often used when describing a low-functioning individual. The average American imagines a man wrapping his house in tin foil to protect against radiation or a transient lying on the sidewalk talking to himself. A psychotic disorder doesn't need to present itself this way, however.

Delusions often feature prominently in psychotic disorders. Simply put, a delusion is a fixed false belief that runs counter to reality. Persecutory delusions are the most common: We all know someone who insists that the world is out to get him. Fear is not a required component of a delusion but often accompanies it. In clinical terms, this is called a paranoid delusion.

It is not necessary to be a non-functioning psychiatric inpatient to suffer from a delusional disorder. Many people go about their lives working, traveling, and even raising a family while maintaining a delusional thought process. All delusions, though, are by definition irrational. This is what makes them pathologic. The harm they bring to the individual who holds them comes from a diminished capacity to live with reality.

They are also impervious to reason; otherwise, they would simply be wrong-headed opinions that change once confronted with reality. As I tell my patients, learning to live with reality—whatever that may be—is a necessary component of growth and emotional health. Failing in that task bodes a poor outcome for the patient.

When a number of associated delusions organize themselves into an irrational belief system, a state of psychosis can develop. When the man who believes the world is out to get him also insists that his restaurant food is poisoned, that his wife is having a lesbian affair with the neighbor's daughter, and that his boss is somehow involved in both—he is psychotic.

He may still be able to function quite well despite this, insisting that he be allowed to bring his own food with him when eating out, for example. Those around him may consider his behavior to be odd, but what if every diner in the restaurant brought his own food with him? Would that behavior still be considered odd? What if every restaurant insisted that customers brought their own food with them "to ensure everyone's safety?" The one patron choosing to instead order from the menu would be seen as irresponsible and even dangerous.

At its core, this is no different than wearing a mask, something we now insist on in schools, restaurants, gyms, and grocery stores from Los Angeles to New York City. Individual mental health problems can thus transform into a truly societal illness.

As I continued to observe my patients and the people around me, it became undeniable that a shared state of irrationality had arisen from the underlying pandemic of fear. In short, everyone had apparently agreed to go crazy at the same time. This mass delusional psychosis, as I began to call it in my public talks, was rooted in fear but organized around a perverse worship of safety. To secure that safety, no sacrifice was too great: canceling graduation and prom, depriving individuals of their ability to make a living, masking children, banning Easter, ordering ailing nursing home patients to die alone and then prohibiting their grieving family members from holding funerals.

This movement had been brewing for some time in the US, with society's elevation of physical safety and self-esteem over mastery, accomplishment, and truth. Mothers no longer allow their children to walk unaccompanied to school. Trophies are given solely for participation. Safe spaces have become ubiquitous at universities, so that students "triggered" by reality have the opportunity to regress developmentally rather than confront unpleasant truths. What changed in 2020 was the expansion of this movement into every facet of public life and the codification of social policy into actual law.

When I would challenge individual patients on their support for this new social order, they could never provide a rationale. Their defense was largely emotional: "I don't feel comfortable...I need to feel safe...I'm too anxious not to." Whenever I would offer objective information to reassure them that their beliefs were misinformed and that their behaviors were not only unnecessary but harmful to themselves and others, they would largely refuse to accept the truth of what I had told them. They had already convinced themselves of a bizarre worldview, with a degree of religiosity I had only previously encountered in hospitalized psychiatric patients.

The mother of a twelve-year-old girl I was seeing for ADHD, for example, would no longer bring her daughter to my office for medication follow-up visits. She had sequestered her in their palatial home in Mandeville Canyon, home to Arnold Schwarzenegger and other wealthy celebrities, only allowing her to leave the house for equestrian practice. Worse, only certain friends were allowed to come to the house to play, and only in the backyard. "When I found out that some of them were living with parents who weren't being careful, I wasn't comfortable with having them over anymore." When I asked what she meant by not "being careful," she explained that these families were not wearing masks outside. Nothing I said could dissuade her from her belief that her daughter was at substantial risk of serious illness and death, in addition to being a vector for disease that could invade their hillside estate.

I quickly despaired of attempting to educate them. It seemed they didn't want to know the truth. Tragically, they appeared fully invested in their delusional belief system and acknowledged having no desire to reconsider it. Like members of a cult who have turned their backs on family, friends, and society, they preferred this new life to the old one.

What had caused this mass delusional psychosis? It certainly wasn't a virus. The only people who were developing serious illness or dying in significant numbers were already sick, old, or both. Meanwhile, the social contagion of psychotic thinking and behavior had spread throughout the population, sparing no demographic. It did appear less prevalent, though, in rural America and among those who described themselves as politically conservative.

This difference was reflected in the largely divergent government responses at the state level (New York vs. Florida or California vs. Texas) and within states (San Francisco vs. Fresno or Miami vs. Tallahassee). New York and California instituted the quickest and most severe lockdowns in the country, while Florida and Texas remained largely open. In-person instruction for grades

K-12 resumed in fall 2020 throughout Florida, while it took California Governor Gavin Newsom another full year to even consider the idea. As Los Angeles County moved to restrict all restaurants to take-out food service in May 2020, adjacent lesser-populated Ventura County remained open for outdoor dining.

It is no secret that throughout the United States today, liberals largely control the cities, while more conservative Americans predominate in the suburbs and rural areas, and the politicians they elect reflect their social preferences. As a consequence, government policies toward the pandemic followed a predictable pattern: Democrat-controlled cities and states largely followed the fast and hard lockdown approach, while the response by Republicans trended toward greater liberty and personal choice. Based on this, it would be reasonable to conclude that, as a group, liberals prefer the promise of safety to liberty, even when those promises cannot be supported by rational arguments. Conservatives, on the other hand, are far more willing to assume personal risk to retain the power to make their own choices.

In short, it appeared that irrational thinking predominated in urban, liberal locales. What forces were at play that conspired to produce such fear-driven, handicapped thinking?

Mass delusional psychosis may be an unfamiliar term, but it is not a new phenomenon. Scottish Journalist Charles Mackey described it in his publication *Extraordinary Popular Delusions and the Madness of Crowds* in 1841, citing the example of the Dutch tulip mania of the early 17th century and the Western European witch mania of the 16th and 17th centuries. In the 20th century, the German and Japanese people developed an ultranationalist hysteria based on racist ideology and used it to commit some of the worst atrocities in human history, as well as launch a world war.

Domestically, the post-WWII Red Scare arose following an increase in subversive actions of foreign and leftist elements in the United States. (One popular delusion from this time was the notion that the Soviets were somehow behind the fluoridation of the American water supply.) Although the concern of domestic espionage by American citizens on behalf of the Soviet Union was not unfounded, fear rapidly evolved into a hysterical overreach with President Truman's 1947 Loyalty Order mandating that all federal employees be subject to scrutiny for their political affiliations. In this case, personal liberty was sacrificed on the altar of domestic security. With the rise of Joe McCarthy, this paranoid insistence on finding Communists under every bed had devastating consequences for the lives of many individuals, regardless of their innocence or guilt.

Fear of disease or infection is a particularly insidious kind of fear, present in humans for thousands of years. Perhaps because the source of disease is invisible, it has the power to overtake reason and develop into a special kind of shared panic. For example, although the AIDS epidemic was real and carried a mortality rate of 100 percent for those infected, the threat to the general population was wildly exaggerated. Yet much of America was paralyzed for several years by the fear of contracting AIDS, in the same way it has been for the past eighteen months due to the Wuhan virus.

In the pandemic of 2020, fear arose from multiple quarters. Intriguingly, however, this fear did not affect everyone in the same way. The Pew Research Center's survey from February 2021 showed that American women were 50 percent more likely than men to report suffering "high levels of psychological distress," including anxiety, insomnia, and "a physical reaction when thinking about the pandemic." The prevalence of distress was increased in younger women age eighteen to twenty-nine, especially young unmarried women, over a third of whom reported high levels of distress. Of all ethnic groups, white women reported the second-highest levels of distress after Hispanic women.

People who feel a lack of agency over their own safety often resort to aggressive attempts to control those around them. Given that, the appearance of the "Karen" phenomenon in American society was not all that surprising. Countless videos were uploaded to social media showing angry, hysterical women screaming at others for not wearing a mask, often chasing them and even physically attacking them.

Women's fear of catching a viral illness not only manifested in public attacks on individuals. It also led to demands for stronger measures and more social controls. I was genuinely shocked to discover many women supporting school closures and masks for children. They justified their positions by saying, "We need to keep our children safe." Despite a total lack of scientific evidence that either measure kept a single child safe, keeping children indoors soothed these women's anxiety.

I heard this frequently in my practice: "We're staying safe by keeping the kids home—it makes me feel more comfortable this way." Several families in my practice with the financial means to do so relocated to summer homes out of state, where the parents could continue to work remotely while keeping the children away from the "dangerous virus." Not one of these families had ever moved away during flu season when influenza kills more children annually than the Wuhan virus has for eighteen months and is far more transmissible from children to adults. Their decision-making was not based on science and reason—it was driven entirely by fear.

I also found that, in most cases, the more emotionally driven the wife was in her insistence on instituting irrational constraints on the family, the more passive and accommodating the husband was in his stance toward his wife. This manifested most often in parents' approaches toward their children, particularly where it involved education and social activities. Mothers generally take the role of activity organizer and school liaison in a family. In 2020 their role shifted to that of safety protocol enforcer, with very little pushback from their husbands.

Many men privately admitted that their wives had become overprotective to the point of paranoia. By and large, however, they were reluctant to challenge them. It was far easier to simply go along with the fear-driven program, even when that meant the children suffered a significant decline in emotional functioning. When I would point out how the new program was largely responsible for the worsening symptoms I saw in my practice, the mother would insist that safety was paramount and what was needed for the children was a medication adjustment rather than a return to normal life. In most cases, the father would agree. Life was hard enough at home—why make it worse by antagonizing the wife?

Meanwhile, with everyone stuck at home in front of a screen, media had a captive audience. That audience was already fearful, and it is human nature to seek out emotionally driven content that resonates with your current emotional state. Every day, print, cable, and online news media made a point to announce how many more people had tested positive, been hospitalized, or died of the virus. Every day the running tally would increase. There was never any mention of preventive measures one could take against infection, other than fear-reinforcing behaviors such as mask-wearing and social isolation. Nor was there any mention of outpatient treatment options unless they were being attacked as ineffective and dangerous.

These attacks began in early 2020 with hydroxychloroquine, a fifty-year-old medication that had been used safely and effectively throughout the world to prevent malaria in infants, pregnant and breast-feeding women, and the elderly. Any positive news of hope from this treatment was ridiculed, and fearful behaviors were reinforced with constant reminders that one was "safer at home," that "masks save lives," and that we should all "do our part, by staying apart," as LA Mayor Eric Garcetti was fond of repeating. By focusing not on real news but instead promoting isolation and fear, American media guaranteed an audience eager to have its hysteria reinforced by terrifying statistics and despairing predictions of mass death.

Public officials also suffered from the effects of the pandemic of fear, but theirs was a special type of fear that stemmed from their sense of responsibility. Fearing they might make the wrong decision and be blamed for unnecessary deaths, when faced with a choice between enabling personal responsibility and instituting more government control, they would nearly always follow the path that offered more protection from public criticism. This meant that rather than underreact, they tended to overreact.

When rates of infection began to rise again in the winter of 2020 in Los Angeles, despite the county's own evidence that showed minimal contribution of viral spread from restaurant traffic, the board of supervisors voted to end all outdoor dining. Politically, this sort of decision had no downside: If fewer people died, the decision would be credited with saving lives; if more people died, the decision would be credited with limiting the number of lives lost.

In the short term, there is no real political benefit for relaxing restrictions in a crisis. The cost to the public, though, is significant—greater and greater fear. With the announcement of more restrictions, it also becomes harder for individual voices of reason to be heard. Restrictions embolden the hysterical, validating their fears. A vicious cycle ensues, one that becomes nearly impossible to halt, much less reverse. Many people now appear to be addicted to the daily drama of fear and the power it confers on hysterical and angry individuals, irresponsible media outlets, and overweening public officials.

One year later, we find ourselves so advanced down this path that we may not be able to recover. We may soon become a marginally functioning society of traumatized individuals, unable to undertake the daily risks necessary to sustain life. The Brown University Department of Pediatrics has found that babies born after January 1, 2020 show an IQ point loss of twenty points, presumably caused by the deprivation of home confinement and universal mask-wearing that impeded normal brain development. Where will we be ten years from now? Is our fate to become like the future America of the 2006 movie *Idiocracy*, where all scientific progress has halted—even reversed—as the population clings to superstitious beliefs and groupthink, wasting their lives in front of mindless online entertainment?

It is my diagnosis that we are suffering from a society-wide mental health crisis due to a pandemic of fear. This affliction requires urgent treatment.

Can it be done? Can our society be cured of its delusional psychosis? Perhaps. The solution, though, will require both a new understanding of how this pandemic began and a profound change in the behavior of all Americans.

Chapter 1

The Terrorization of Women: A Brief Cultural History

THERE IS A REASON why the name "Karen" was chosen to describe people who accost strangers and shame them for "unsafe" behaviors such as standing too close or not wearing a mask outdoors: Those people are overwhelmingly women.

In the summer of 2020, I was invited to attend an informal gathering in a neighbor's driveway. A professional musician, the neighbor wanted to lift the spirits of everyone on the block by offering a recital with her classical music performance group. It sounded lovely. When I arrived, though, I saw that the entire audience was wearing masks—outdoors. The way they had arranged their chairs, it was also clear they wanted to be far apart from one another. The musicians themselves (all women) were also sitting far apart from one another and also wearing masks. The group leader informed me that I would need to stand somewhere away from the driveway unless I wore a mask.

I could sense that my mere presence was making many of the women there uncomfortable—all because I chose to breathe freely and not cover my face with a ceremonial piece of cloth. The entire affair resembled a cult meeting, where all reason had been banished. In its place was a worship of fear. I chose to leave after a few songs, as the experience became unpleasant and not at all uplifting. For this frightened group of women, an outdoor neighborhood concert had become a potential super-spreader event.

What was clear to me was that fear and anxiety had driven these women to attempt to control everyone around them.

Wearing a mask outdoors has always been irrefutably irrational. There is no evidence that any significant number of people have caught a respiratory infection by being outdoors. To defy all reason and common sense and demand that those around you follow suit is simply tyrannical. This behavior stems from emotional instability and hysteria, not from a reasonable concern for health and safety. Social norms used to contain intrusive overreach into the decision-making of others when it did not infringe onto your basic rights. No more. In the name of safety, any order is justified and not subject to questioning.

This new drive to control others appears to be driven by fear—and it is also propelled largely by women. As the 2020 Pew Survey revealed, there is a substantial difference in anxiety levels between men and women today, especially young, unmarried women. This raises the question: Why are they so afraid?

That women are more anxious and fearful than men is a provocative statement. It may be condemned as insensitive or even misogynistic. The majority of my patients are women, however, and I am committed to their welfare. My work involves helping them improve their emotional and psychological functioning. Yet just as male and female bodies differ in their relative risks of physical disease, from my clinical training and experience, I know that male and female psychologies differ, too. The Pew study may at first appear bewildering, but the results begin to make sense when those real male and female differences are honestly assessed and taken into account.

In this chapter, I will explore the roots of this anxiety among American women, which has, by every measure, been growing for decades.

Let's start with basic biological realities. Women, as a sex, are physically smaller and weaker than men; therefore, to some degree, women have good reason to be fearful. Unless she is armed, a woman is at a distinct disadvantage if attacked by a man.

Contrary to what most people believe, though, women are not disproportionately victims of violent crime. As of 2019, in urban centers, men and women were victimized in equal percentages. Living in a suburban or rural area is protective for women, whose rates of victimization are up to one-third lower than they are for men. Crime victims do report, however, being victimized far more frequently by men than by women. Men make up 75 percent of all offenders.

This would account for women feeling disproportionately fearful of men, particularly single women who live in urban areas. As women marry and begin having children, they often relocate to suburban neighborhoods, where crime rates are lower. One would expect, then, that anxiety would be worse for young women living in cities, which is supported by the Pew study.

Men and women differ in other ways, too. Evolutionary psychology has shown there to be significant differences between the personalities of men and women. Numerous studies reveal that women report higher levels of neuroticism, extroversion, agreeableness, and conscientiousness compared to men. Moreover, these differences become apparent early in life and persist into old age. This large body of research shows that male/female differences are not necessarily culturally dependent, nor are they developmentally mediated. These differences reveal themselves in my private practice, where anxiety disorders are far more common in my female patients than in my male patients. Phobic disorders, in particular, present almost exclusively in women.

Women are also more vulnerable due to their higher degree of empathy and attachment to others, especially the most vulnerable. Women have always served as the primary caretakers of infants and children, as well as of elderly parents. The unique attachment a mother develops for her child includes an ever-present fear, to a varying degree, of injury and loss. British psychoanalyst David Winnicott described this most clearly over fifty years ago in his theory of "primary maternal preoccupation." New mothers are biologically conditioned to develop a powerful identification with their babies that supplants every other relationship in her life for some time. This is the main reason fathers often feel left out at home once their baby arrives. Many take this personally and feel rejected by their wives, leading to stress in the marital relationship. In my practice, I explain to new mothers and fathers that the intense focus the mother brings towards her baby is a necessary and healthy one. In fact, it serves a psychological need for the baby's normal development. Even after the period of primary maternal preoccupation ends, generally within the first year of the baby's life, mothers continue to serve a role quite different from that of fathers: They are the immediate protectors of a child's physical and emotional safety. For a new mother, this hyper-focus on her baby is not a weakness but rather a biological necessity, even as it may render her emotionally overprotective and otherwise relationally limited for a time.

As children grow up, their mothers continue to face emotional challenges due to fear and anxiety. School admissions, down to the level of kindergarten or earlier, have become a nearly universal source of anxiety for my female patients. Others invest themselves emotionally in their children's success, and the most accepted measure of success today—for those under age eighteen—is education. The assumption that admission to a competitive school drives future professional achievement and social standing goes unchallenged in most circles. Few parents are aware of the work of Dale and Krueger, who showed in their 2002 and 2011 publications that the selectivity of a school has little to no bearing on professional success. Rather it is the qualities that earned them admission—discipline, intelligence, maturity—that led to their success. Unfortunately, this is lost on most parents.

Overwhelmingly, I find that it is mothers rather than fathers who suffer from impairing anxiety over a child's grades and school admissions, to the point of requiring medication to cope with the worry. This has led some parents I know who put their children's health at risk by agreeing to comply with experimental vaccine mandates to maintain enrollment at LA's prestigious private schools.

Of course, the fact that more women than men call on me for help with their anxiety disorder could simply be due to a filtering bias. Perhaps women are more likely than men to seek professional help with emotional illness. That does not appear to be the reason why anxiety disorders in my practice predominate in women, however. The research in this field has been remarkably consistent. Women have been shown to be significantly more phobic than men, for example. In one study of nearly 27,000 women across cultures, women displayed nearly double the prevalence of generalized anxiety and panic disorder compared with men. Greater susceptibility to fear, then—both rational and otherwise—appears to be a natural consequence of being a woman.

Biology and psychology alone, though, cannot fully explain why women today suffer from such a disparity of fear and anxiety compared with men. Women have always been mothers. They have always had to protect their children from danger. Their relative physical weakness and vulnerability to physical harm from men have remained constant throughout time. By any objective measure, women are physically safer now than they have ever been, with violent crime rates at all-time lows in most cities through the end of 2019.

Has something changed in the environment to amplify women's fears? Has there been a cultural evolution that has magnified an intrinsic biological and psychological predisposition to female anxiety? Just consider some of the profound societal changes in the United States since WWII.

With the end of the war in 1945, the United States began a period of unsurpassed economic growth. But this period of peace and prosperity did not last long. The '50s brought fears of Communist infiltration and overarching nuclear anxiety, as people built bomb shelters in their backyards, and children were subjected to frightening (and ultimately pointless) duck and cover drills.

Domestic unrest swept the country in the 1960s as the Vietnam War, the civil rights movement, the murder of a president, urban riots, and campus unrest shattered the illusion of national unity.

The 1970s brought fears of environmental collapse and even the extinction of the human race. Since the first Earth Day on April 22, 1970, this sense of impending doom has only gotten worse, with a series of panics about overpopulation, ozone depletion, peak oil, global warming, extreme weather events, deforestation, nuclear energy disasters, mass species extinction, poisoning by agricultural chemicals, electromagnetic and cell phone radiation, and rising sea levels that are predicted to drown American cities.

Women have been particularly vulnerable to these successive panics. Indeed, some women have internalized this fear to such an extent that they now proclaim they no longer wish to have children. There is even a name for these women: BirthStrikers.

One of the most prominent environmental activists today is an eighteen-year-old Swedish woman named Greta Thunberg. This poster child for environmental awareness and activism has since childhood suffered from multiple mental illnesses, including panic disorder, obsessive-compulsive disorder, and anorexia. She also claims to be autistic. Her famously impassioned speech before the United Nations in 2019 excoriating world leaders for their "betrayal" of young people over climate change revealed her to be emotionally unstable and irrational.

Alexandria Ocasio Cortez (AOC), at age twenty-nine the youngest woman ever to serve in Congress, apparently agrees, as she promised in 2019 that "The world is gonna end in twelve years if we don't address climate change."

Despite substantial criticism of these absolutist positions by respected scientists, Thunberg and AOC continue to be held up as symbols of courage whose views merit serious consideration by world leaders. Anyone who criticizes their positions is derided as "anti-science" and worse. AOC frequently rejects any criticism of her positions as "sexist." Bjørn Lomborg, director of the Copenhagen Consensus Center, has been labeled a misogynist for daring to challenge Thunberg's catastrophic proclamations of environmental apocalypse. In the environmentalist movement, neurotic and hysterical women must be treated with kid gloves, given a pass, and certainly never held to the same standards as men. In this way, their fear continues to grow and infects the broader society.

Meanwhile, several generations of American women—the freest and most affluent women in history—have been persuaded that ours is a country that "hates" them and seeks to drive them back into patriarchal subjugation. The rise of the pro-life movement after the 1974 *Roe v Wade* decision was touted by feminists as evidence of a desire to control women's bodies and force them into dangerous back-alley abortions. Any man who advocates for restricting abortion in any way—particularly for religious reasons—is deemed a misogynist. During the Trump administration, Hollywood touted a theocratic "Handmaid's Tale" dystopia that captured the hearts of liberal women. Planned Parenthood exploited this manufactured fear in its staged protests outside the US Capital in 2017, its protesters costumed in red robes with white cones over their heads. "Women's bodies, futures, and lives are literally on the line," one said.

September 11, 2001 brought Islamic terror to the US and took the lives of 3,000 Americans. Multiple studies and surveys published post-9/11 noted that women, in addition to being more fearful in general compared with men, were especially fearful of future attacks. Terrorism is a particularly insidious source of fear, as it can strike anywhere, at any time. After twenty years, TSA rules still require passengers to remove all liquids from carry-on bags and take off their shoes, serving as a permanent reminder of this ever-present threat.

In addition, women—particularly liberal women—must now contend with the scourge of white supremacy, neo-Nazis, and systemic racism. Reportedly, hate crimes reached an all-time high in 2020, and the current President has declared white supremacists to be "the most lethal terrorist threat" to the US today.

There is very little evidence that these threats are real. Over the past twenty years, the total number of hate crime reports has not significantly changed. What has changed is who is committing them and against whom. Racially motivated hate crimes against blacks are declining, while religiously motivated hate crimes, primarily against Jews, have dramatically increased. Moreover, the perpetrators of anti-Jewish hate crimes are predominantly black, as are those of the recently sensationalized anti-Asian hate crimes in urban areas scattered throughout the United States.

There is also no evidence to support the belief that white supremacy is a significant problem in the US today. Neither is there evidence to support the presence of systemic racism. Racism exists, but its power is weak, and the social pressure against it is overwhelming.

A related bogeyman pushed by media to frighten Americans is the phenomenon of mass shootings. Guns in general have been vilified by Democrats and liberal activists for many years. Despite all evidence to the contrary, legal gun owners are frequently blamed for crimes committed using guns in the US when, in fact, it is illegally owned guns that are used in the commission of crimes in nearly all cases. Americans with concealed carry permits are perhaps the most law-abiding group of Americans, with a felony conviction rate well below that of police officers.

Yet in a misguided effort to ensure "safety," a nationwide movement is afoot to make all guns illegal and to create "gun-free zones" in schools, malls, parks, and other public places. In every place where gun ownership has been severely restricted or banned, murder rates have increased. When gang-related violence is excluded, the number of mass shootings in the US has remained largely flat over the past twenty years.

Gun-free zones do not increase safety, either—they attract crime. 95 percent of all shootings in the US occur in places where it is illegal for a civilian to carry a gun. Between 1950 and 2010, not a single mass shooting occurred in an area where general civilians are allowed to carry a gun.

In sum, the argument to limit or eliminate legal gun ownership, and the push to outlaw the right of legal gun owners to carry weapons in public places, is irrational and not supported by statistics. The unfortunate result is that women, who are disproportionately affected by violent crime, have grown more fearful due to years of being told that they and their children are at high risk of being shot in a public place by a man—usually an "angry white man"—carrying a legal firearm.

All these fears—and many more that we could cite—were avidly promoted by American mass media, almost as though there was a concerted campaign to inculcate a baseline of fear and anxiety in American women.

It's working: Americans, in general, are far more anxious and fearful than at any time since such measurements began. And women disproportionately suffer its effects. Over the course of their lives, nearly one in three Americans will be diagnosed with an anxiety disorder. Women, however, are 50 percent more likely to be diagnosed than men. In 2010, greater than 10 percent of all American women were prescribed anti-anxiety medication, a rate double that of men.

In 2011, alarmed by these statistics, *The Guardian* asked, "Are women crazy?" Ten years later, the numbers did not budge. By comparison, thirty years ago—hardly the dark ages in terms of mental health awareness and treatment—less than 4 percent of American women were prescribed anti-anxiety medication.

In the category of eating disorders (anorexia and bulimia), lifetime prevalence more than doubled between the period of 2000–2006 and the period 2013–2018, to 9 percent. Women still make up the majority of patients diagnosed with an eating disorder, despite recent increases in prevalence in young men. Most of these women are white, well-educated, and well-off. This demographic appears to be the most susceptible to developing an eating disorder, a psychiatric illness that is, at its core, an anxiety disorder marked by fear, a delusional view of one's own physical appearance, and poor coping skills. The pandemic of fear in American women is clinically measurable.

Now comes a highly contagious, lethal virus let loose on the world from a lab in Wuhan, China, that has saturated every inch of America. Bewilderingly, as death rates continue to decline, the public demand for universal masking—including that of children—simply increases. This makes no rational sense, even for those who mistakenly believe that masks prevent the transmission of respiratory viruses.

One would assume those people would feel quite safe wearing a mask, as they believe that it protects them from getting sick. On the contrary, they are the most ferocious group in their attacks on those who choose not to wear masks. This has been revealed most clearly with the arrival of the India strain—known as the "Delta variant." Many school districts have re-instituted mask mandates for students, some as young as two years old. Surprisingly, despite a complete absence of evidence that children are at any appreciable risk of serious illness or that masking children provides any health benefit, many parents fully support these mandates.

I recently advised Florida Governor Ron DeSantis in a public roundtable forum to prohibit all K-12 school mask mandates in the state based on lack of evidence of benefit and substantial evidence of harm to children. Since my statement was broadcast locally and repeated on national news, I have been inundated with phone calls, email messages, and social media comments from hysterical and angry parents accusing me of "murdering children" and threatening to report me to the state medical board for malpractice. The majority of these people are women.

Clearly, over the past decade, American women have been struck by a pandemic of anxiety. Given what they have been taught about the world they live in, how could they not be? From a young age, they must cope with a patriarchal culture that seeks to enslave and exploit them. College campuses are nothing more than rape spaces, and the office is swimming in sexual harassment. Meanwhile, racist men with guns are lying in wait, looking for any opportunity to assault them or murder their children at school. The planet is being poisoned by rapacious capitalists, and terrorists may blow us out of the sky at any moment.

Meanwhile, in the aftermath of the 2020 George Floyd riots, white liberal women appeared to think it was their personal responsibility to make amends for 400 years of slavery, segregation, and racial inequality. It has been widely remarked—not least by blacks themselves— that liberal white women have embraced the cause of social justice with a fervor that can only be explained by an agonizing sense of guilt about their "privilege." No wonder they were primed to explode in a paroxysm of rage and fear after a year of unnecessary lockdowns.

This brief excursion into cultural history shows that in addition to their natural propensity to feel vulnerable and in need of protection, American women have been subjected to a vicious decades-long campaign of terrorization that could not have been more effective had it been planned by a sinister cabal of misogynistic geniuses.

There is, in truth, only one thing that might have helped them avoid this state of clinical pathology—and it is the very thing which, ironically, they have been taught to fear above all: namely, the men in their lives.

Traditionally, as everyone knows, it has been the role of men to calm and ground women's fears, not the role of doctors but of fathers, uncles, brothers, and, of course, husbands. As science amply shows, men are evolved for the good of the species to adopt a protective attitude toward females, and this innate proclivity is powerfully reinforced by millennia of social and religious conditioning in every known society on earth. No society exists where women are left to fend for themselves. Men are evolved and socialized to love, provide for, and protect their women.

This may be an unpopular view among liberal white women themselves, but it is not so controversial among women of traditional working class, religious, or foreign backgrounds. Among Christian and Jewish couples, according to the Deseret News, "When it comes to marriage, women are most satisfied if they are half of a religious couple embracing traditional gender roles." In my own experience, the more religious the couple, the truer this is.

Before beginning my private practice in West Los Angeles, where the majority of my adult patients are financially secure and hold a college degree, I worked with low-income and immigrant families at an LA County Department of Mental Health outpatient clinic on the Harbor Hospital campus in the city of Carson. The differences regarding expectations in gender roles between mothers and fathers were striking. Regardless of employment status, I found that women consistently expected their male partners to provide for their physical safety. This was not an insignificant request, given the high crime rates where many of my patients' families lived.

It was only after leaving the Harbor clinic for an entirely different patient demographic in private practice that I began to see how these expectations changed among native-born, secular, professional Americans. In particular, many women in this demographic take tremendous pride in being "independent" and not "needing" a man, even when married. They rarely express a desire to their husband or partner for protection. The more they do on their own, the more successful they feel.

My suggesting that they surrender even a portion of their autonomy to their husband to achieve greater security would be viewed, at best, as an odd recommendation, and, at worst, as an insult to their capacities as women to survive on their own.

Unfortunately, while the cultural terrorization of women described above proceeded unchecked, there was a parallel change in relationships between men and women brought about by feminism. Originally a liberal movement aimed at providing more freedom and opportunity for women, feminism evolved into a more radical movement that peddled a negative view of men as tyrants and toxic abusers.

It is to this issue we now turn to understand why during the pandemic American men failed so dismally in their duty to provide a sense of safety and security for the women in their lives—with consequences that have affected every one of us.

Chapter 2

Dereliction of Duty: How Feminized American Men Failed Their Women

I N LATE 2020, a woman was overhead commenting on how she felt leaving her house every morning and seeing men, both alone and with their wives, walking on the street with masks covering their faces: "This does not make me feel safe. On the contrary, it scares me. If I were married to one of these men, what would he do the moment a real threat appears? He would throw me under the bus and run for the hills. I'd be left to fend for myself."

Her view is not an isolated one. Hundreds of women across the United States have reported the same experience to me directly.

For over a year, I have been traveling the country and speaking before audiences of Americans hungry for truth. They are bewildered and confused, and many feel they have been let down by those in positions of authority and influence—including the medical profession, the national media, and our political leaders. But many women express a more personal concern, one that is focused on their partners and that mingles feelings of impatience, disappointment, and outright contempt.

Whenever I talk about the emasculation of American men, I see heads start to nod. Without fail, at the end of every talk, a number of women come up to thank me for calling out one of their greatest concerns. These women struggle to put into words what they have been feeling very strongly for many years—a loss of masculinity in the American man.

"Where have all the men gone?" one young single woman asked me. Another pointed out that her son refuses to move out of the house—at age twenty-four—because he fears embarking on an independent life. A married woman opposed to her children wearing masks complained that her husband told her to "shut up about the masks at school" because he doesn't want "the family to get in trouble."

In short, these women recognize that American men have been rendered all but useless to them in a crisis. Women know this instinctively because they rely on men for physical security. This instinct transcends politics and culture—it is biological. Conservative women tend to know and understand this intellectually and are more or less at peace with it. But liberal women often suffer cognitive dissonance between their feminist philosophy that tells them they do not need men to be happy and their timeless biological necessities.

I see this split when I speak at churches, primarily Christian evangelical churches. All the women congregants are religious conservatives. When they speak to me after my talk, they indicate how my words and ideas closely align with their religious views. On the other hand, liberal women in my clinical practice often struggle to accept that much of their emotional pain comes from pursuing a feminist approach to male-female relationships, one where it is the woman who should express strength, while the man is largely superfluous outside his role of remaining agreeable and emotionally supportive. Political orientation thus plays a critical role in how women develop their expectations of men.

Regardless of where a woman falls on the political spectrum, however, her emotional stability suffers when she feels unsafe. For this reason, today's feminized American men do not typically play their traditional role, which is to ground and contain women's anxiety in a crisis. Instead, they amplify it.

According to women themselves, it is the expression of masculinity that provides comfort to women. A woman I know who recently began a new relationship learned that the man knows how to use a gun and keeps one at home. "I hate guns," she told me, "but when he told me that, it made me feel safe." He had demonstrated to her that he possesses the skills and the tools to protect her. This quality is becoming increasingly rare.

When I work with male patients, I often discover that they have no idea how to express anger. This is because they tend to confuse healthy aggression with rage and destruction. They go through life—and their relationships with women—suppressing these healthy and normal feelings, choosing to remain silent when conflicts arise, inhibited from taking appropriate and necessary action during a crisis. Only when I explain to them that setting boundaries with others and defending them assertively and forcefully is essential for their own health and the health of their relationships do they realize why they continue to fall short in those relationships.

One patient I've been working with for years had been stuck in a never-ending series of arguments with his long-time girlfriend. When he moved into a new house by himself, his girlfriend felt scared about being left out. So she insisted on making all the decisions about how the house would be furnished and decorated. Initially, he allowed her to take over, but I could clearly see this was not only upsetting him but also adding to the tension and discord in their relationship, bordering on resentment on his part.

On my suggestion, he stood up to her and firmly said, "No. I understand my moving into a new house makes you uncomfortable and may even scare you, but I will be deciding how to furnish my home. If I need your help, I'll ask for it." She backed down, let him take the lead, and returned to a more supportive role of offering suggestions only when asked for them.

The expression of anxiety is, for women, often a plea for help, a request for the man in her life to step up and take action. When a man remains inert and defers decision-making to the woman, her anxiety worsens, often converting to hysteria and unwanted efforts at control. In other words, much of the time, so-called "controlling" women are simply reacting to a vacuum of male assertiveness in anxious or fearful situations.

Two generations ago, a woman would still turn to her husband and other men to fight threats, protect her and her children, and offer reassurance and security. She could then focus on her own physical and emotional well-being and that of her dependents. Not anymore. Her inability to do this today is largely the fault of men themselves and their acceptance of emasculation.

The stigmatizing and decline of traditional masculinity has had disastrous consequences for both men and women and their relationships with one another. Perhaps the most recent damaging effect has been a vacuum of male courage in American society. In 2017, over 7 million American men aged twenty-five through fifty-four were living in their parents' basement, not working and not looking for work. They had retreated from the world to avoid facing the threat of failure and rejection.

To protect themselves from the unavoidable, they have paid a psychological price—weakness. Their numbers continue to rise. In fact, the presence of homebound and unproductive children is one of the most common complaints I receive from parents. "My child graduated from college two years ago, doesn't work, still lives at home, and won't leave."

Adult dependency is not limited to single men, either. Married men suffer from a similar passivity and self-victimization in their relationships with their wives. Despite holding clear views on finance, health, and childrearing, many husbands and fathers in my practice often admit that they do not confront their wives when there is a difference of opinion. When I ask why, the typical response is, "It's not worth it," or "I'd rather just let it go and move on."

As a result, they often feel ineffectual. Their sexual virility suffers. They become resentful. By failing to display courage in their marriage, they have defined themselves as men who will not fight for what they believe in and matters to them. This lack of courage expands into all other aspects of their lives: childrearing, work, and even self-care. A man who lacks courage lacks self-respect, and a man who does not respect himself cannot effectively engage with women.

The vacuum of male courage in our society has been growing for many years, but it recently made possible the societal hysteria that led to a mass delusional psychosis disproportionately affecting women.

By all measures, American men have been feminized. This is not a metaphor. Testosterone levels in men have been dropping for decades since at least 1987. Even after accounting for age, smoking, and obesity, the decline persists. The average drop has been about 1 percent per year, meaning that a sixty-year-old man in 2004 had testosterone levels 17 percent lower than of a sixty-year-old man in 1987. The actual causes are still unknown, but many believe that greater exposure to environmental toxins, such as pesticides and chemicals common in household products, are to blame.

This trend has very likely been exacerbated by economic shifts. With a decrease in demand for manual labor, more men have been pursuing careers in desk jobs that require no physical strength or movement. Here's an intriguing statistic: In 2016, researchers found a significant drop in grip strength in male millennials age twenty to thirty-four, from an average of 117 pounds of grip force in 1985 to only 98 pounds in 2016. Surprisingly, grip-strength loss was also detected in women. Loss of muscle mass is associated with lower testosterone levels. Is it at all surprising that between 2000 and 2013 the use of supplemental testosterone in men has skyrocketed?

Moreover, during this time, women have increased their representation in higher education and professions previously dominated by men, such as law, medicine, and business. With a greater supply of workers, wages have been driven down as men now face increased competition from women entering the workforce. This undermines the confidence and self-esteem of men and confuses them as to their proper role in women's lives.

Societal views of masculinity have substantially changed as well. Two Pew Research Center polls taken in 2017 and 2019 reveal several important ones. Only 31 percent of men viewed themselves as "very masculine," with white men in the lowest subgroup at only 28 percent. The more educated the man—a four-year college degree or higher level of education—the less masculine he felt.

Also, views on masculinity appear to track with political orientation. While 49 percent of Republican men view themselves as very masculine, only 23 percent of Democrat men do. And while 78 percent of Republican men view masculinity as a good thing, only 49 percent of Democrats do. Perhaps not surprisingly, the poll also found that younger women do not view themselves as especially feminine—only 19 percent of millennials compared to 36 percent of boomers. White educated Democrat men do not see themselves as masculine or value masculinity in society, while young women as a whole do not see themselves as feminine.

Meanwhile, married women who work full-time understandably expect their husbands to shoulder a greater share of domestic work, including child-rearing responsibilities that previously fell under the exclusive domain of mothers. This has given rise to a huge amount of social commentary and a raft of therapeutic books that attempt to address the problem, from Joshua Coleman's *The Lazy Husband: How to Get Men to Do More Parenting and Housework* to Eve Rodsky's *Fair Play: A Game-Changing Solution to When You Have Too Much to Do.*

However, some female authors have continued to champion the "all-in" model of career and mothering, such as Sheryl Sandberg's book *Lean In* and Amy Chua's memoir *Battle Hymn of the Tiger Mother*, which exalt the working woman's capacity to simultaneously succeed at the highest level professionally and maintain a full-time, hands-on role as both mother and micromanager of the lives of her children.

The result of these cultural changes has been catastrophic for the mental health of both men and women. Although part-time work has long been found to have a beneficial effect on the psychological well-being of married women, a 2018 US Census report shows that two-thirds of working mothers have been working fulltime. This appears to have led to increased stress and greater marital conflict. Men married to women who earn more than they do report feeling less fulfilled. In 2017, *Harvard Business Review* published research revealing that wives who held higher status positions than their husbands were more likely to feel resentful or embarrassed, leading to less marital satisfaction and increasing the likelihood of divorce.

The Quarterly Journal of Economics published similar findings in 2015, noting, "In couples where the wife earns more than the husband, the wife spends more time on household chores; moreover, those couples are less satisfied with their marriage and are more likely to divorce." Furthermore, as the American Sociological Review reported in 2012, when a married man's share of traditionally female domestic chores increases, couples have less frequent sex. The unfortunate consequence has been a disproportionate number of divorce filings by women: Between 2009 and 2015, women initiated 69 percent of all divorces. Among college-educated women, that number rises to a staggering 90 percent.

Clearly, most women are not happy with the contemporary redefining of traditional gender roles in male-female relationships. Many are afraid to speak up—intimidated into silence by their fear of being seen as unsupportive of feminist doctrine.

This doctrine began in the 1960s, as Gloria Steinem's popularization of the phrase, "A woman without a man is like a fish without a bicycle," announced to the world feminism's assertion of the irrelevance of men. Unlike the suffragettes of the early 20th century who fought for equal voting rights, post-WWII feminism, with its successive waves, each more radical than the last, quickly came to reject equality under the law and instead sought to rewrite the entire social contract.

For the past twenty years, feminists have increasingly taught young women the virtues of competing with men rather than partnering with them. Instead of encouraging women to marry and supporting their natural inclination to raise children, feminists have derided marriage, lauded singledom and single motherhood, and fought for abortion on demand. Where has this taken us?

The rise of feminism empowered women professionally but at the same time changed relations between the sexes in ways that were self-defeating for women and left them more vulnerable than before, with the loss of male protection and respect for female modesty. Many women in the dating market complain that men treat them as sexual objects and send them pornographic pictures in lieu of engaging in traditional courtship. Apparently, proclaiming the sexual empowerment of women has given rise to a culture of diminished expectations where romance is concerned. As women now belatedly discover, this has given men the mistaken impression that women do not need or want to be treated differently.

One especially unfortunate byproduct of contemporary feminism is the false teaching of toxic masculinity. This term has come to mean, essentially, that men—particularly straight white men—are unhealthy, sick, and dangerous to women, children, homosexuals, minorities, immigrants, and anyone else who doesn't conform to their narrow and reactionary norms and expectations. Democrats neatly co-opted this prejudice when they argued that "angry white men" were the driving force behind the elections of George W. Bush and Donald Trump.

What we now know as toxic masculinity has its cultural roots in the 1960s and '70s with the promotion of questionable rape and domestic abuse statistics intended to justify legislation that would increase female protection from violent fathers or husbands—a laudable goal, but one that led to an overgeneralized fear of men and a fixation on what is now called "rape culture." Since then, the presumption has spread that men and boys are inherently violent and need to be completely resocialized.

Healthy expressions of masculinity—strength, assertiveness, the inclination to protect—have all been redefined as universally unhealthy, often dangerous, and certainly unwanted, as the 2019 Pew Research Center poll showed. Any woman in the presence of a man who displays these qualities is expected to resist by challenging his authority and virtue. If he refuses to concede that he has wronged her, then she is encouraged to redefine herself as a victim and announce that he has made her feel unsafe. In response, several generations of American men have undertaken to expunge these formerly admired male characteristics and become fathers, sons, and husbands in a new and much more passive egalitarian mode.

Surprisingly, this misguided movement continues to grow despite attempts by many men to feminize themselves as a way of purging their toxicity. The social conditioning of women to fear masculine men runs counter to evolutionary biology yet flows quite smoothly from modern feminist theory that denigrates men and views them as obstacles to the success, accomplishments, and safety of women.

Rape culture has also been invented by feminists as a rationale for female fear of men. The term is intentionally vague and includes everything from sexually explicit jokes to unwanted kissing to forcible rape. Media frequently report that one in four college students has been sexually assaulted—an alarming statistic. If it were true, it would be hard to imagine any parent allowing their daughter to attend college. Yet it is simply another lie invented to malign and intimidate men and frighten young women.

In reality, rates of sexual assault of all types in the United States have been in decline for years, with college campuses thought to be, in general, safer for women than most other places. One would never know that, though, given the alarming propaganda put out by college administrators advertising "sexual violence" workshops that only serve to remind new female arrivals of the danger lurking in their male counterparts. I frequently hear from my female college student patients how these teach-in sessions have become a common and accepted component of new student orientation.

As part of my new patient interview, I ask about their history of sexual abuse or assault. Many women say they have been sexually abused or assaulted. When I ask for more detail, however, I often hear them describe awkward encounters with men who made clumsy passes or sex acts with men while one or both were intoxicated with alcohol or drugs, leading to regret and embarrassment the following day. These women have been primed to castigate the man involved or displace their own shared responsibility onto him.

This way of thinking, which completely contradicts the feminist teaching of female sexual agency, has turned women into professional victims and men into de facto aggressors. The natural consequence is for women to become fearful of men in general and, specifically, men who express any romantic or sexual interest in them.

Is it simplistic to reduce all this to the effects of feminism? Perhaps. But it is a fair conclusion to state that, essentially, feminist indoctrination has wrecked the bond between men and women, consigning men to a state of perpetual confusion and impotence. As feminism exults in its triumph over men, both sexes lose. Authors Suzanne Venker and Phyllis Schlafly describe in *The Flipside of Feminism* exactly how women have become less happy as they have gained more freedom, more education, and more power. In this view, feminism at its core is actually an anti-female movement founded on grievance ideology that fuels resentment against men while simultaneously exhorting women to discard their femininity in place of more masculine traits such as aggression, competitiveness, and dominance.

It is also a fact that more divorces are initiated these days by restless women seeking greater personal fulfillment. It's a female version of the classic midlife crisis. Instead of working out their problems with the men in their lives, they throw themselves into the dating market in their fifties where they are bitterly disappointed to find that men their age want younger women—and can get them—whereas they must date men older than themselves.

Men who choose to participate in this unnatural and unhealthy crusade find themselves sidelined, with no relevant role to play in their relationships with women. Women emboldened with ersatz courage are then abandoned by the men in their lives to engage in life's battles alone and unsupported. The surrender of real courage by men inevitably produces fearful women, and fearful women channel their fear into controlling others.

I encountered a consequence of this dysfunctional dynamic on a local level in early 2020, when the home-owner's association (HOA) in my neighborhood in Los Angeles closed the nearby park after receiving a report that several small children were seen rolling on the grass. To make the park "safe," the entire ground was sprayed with a disinfectant. The disinfecting of the grass was simply a pretext to close the park, however, because once the spraying had ended, the park remained closed for nearly an entire year.

When it finally re-opened, new regulations appeared on signs posted at the entrance ordering all park visitors to wear masks and banning children from play-ing with one another. Mothers of the children—over-whelmingly upper-middle-class liberal women—dutiful-ly complied. Many voluntarily policed unaccompanied children who violated the new rules and threatened to report them. These women also delighted in scolding the nannies, lesser-educated black or Hispanic women who generally ignored the signs and encouraged the children under their supervision to continue to play freely.

The HOA then sent out a series of email announce-ments shaming residents for violating the rules, warning that the park might need to be closed once again if the violations continued. Security patrols hired by the HOA began harassing visitors and evicting them from the park when they refused to wear masks or stand six feet apart from one another while playing.

As far as I know, no men stepped forward to point out the lunacy of the park closure, the masking and distancing rules, and the coercive tactics encouraged by the HOA. The movement to control was driven exclusively by women, many of them mothers, who defended their fear-driven behavior by repeatedly announcing that they were only trying to protect the safety and wellbeing of the children.

I think it is safe to say that if their husbands had stepped forward to offer a rational, reassuring voice that there was no need to worry, most of the women in the neighborhood would have been able to re-direct their protective instinct toward more traditional, and helpful, mothering. Yet the men remained silent, leaving a void that was quickly filled with female hysteria and rage.

With the near disappearance of courageous men, women's fear and anxiety was amplified by both local and national media, whose concerns no longer lay with reporting news but rather with pushing partisan agendas and capturing as many viewers as possible. In the next chapter, we will consider the role of media and government in amplifying and magnifying the climate of fear to the point where it became a pandemic and, ultimately, a national psychosis.

Chapter 3

Fanning the Flames: The Role of Media and Government

I N MARCH 2020, newspapers and television news programs launched tracking boards, updated daily, that announced the reported cumulative death toll from the Wuhan virus. Early on, evidence suggested these numbers were wildly inflated, as even the CDC noted that only five percent of all deaths attributed to the virus had no additional causes listed on the death certificate. Yet they were reported on page one of printed news and in the opening segment of broadcast news every day for months, providing the false impression that healthy Americans were dying throughout the country in alarming numbers and that the viral pandemic had become the greatest current threat to public health.

Motorcycle accidents, suicides, and even drug overdoses were all categorized as deaths caused by the virus, so long as the victim had a positive nasal swab before, and—in some cases— after death. I spoke with a paramedic in summer 2020 who told me that the day before, he was called upon to help a woman who had overdosed on fentanyl. She was declared dead on arrival at the hospital, with the cause of the death listed as the Wuhan virus. Presumably, her post-mortem nasal swab came back positive. That is obviously not what killed her.

The inflated fatality numbers were also driven by the CDC's convenient change in infectious disease data collection protocol in April 2020 that ensured most influenza and pneumonia deaths became presumptive positive Wuhan virus deaths. Not surprisingly, fewer Americans began dying of pneumonia after that. In many states, when a patient died of pneumonia, it was simply assumed the cause was the Wuhan virus—no confirmatory laboratory testing needed.

Meanwhile, the media embraced this kind of sensationalized and inaccurate reporting for reasons of their own. As discussed earlier, courageous men had largely disappeared. This allowed women's fear and anxiety to be amplified by both local and national media, whose concerns no longer lay with reporting news but rather with pushing partisan agendas (such as defeating Donald Trump in the upcoming presidential election) and capturing as many viewers as possible. Reporting daily death counts and disseminating personal interest stories about alarming, yet highly rare medical tragedies guaranteed ratings would stay high while sapping the will of Americans to re-elect the sitting president. "Fear-porn," as it came to be called, served both the economic and political interests of its purveyors.

Once it became impossible to defend the accuracy of the mortality statistics, as well-respected epidemiologists like Harvey Risch and skeptical journalists like former New York Times science reporter Alex Berenson exposed the corruption in the data, media pivoted to hospitalization rates, which were equally troubled by bias for political and financial gain. For example, Medicare began reimbursing hospitals for any "Covid" diagnosis, offering up to $35,000 in additional payment for patients with that diagnosis who were placed on a ventilator. I personally know several ER physicians and hospitalists who were pressured by hospital management to add "Covid" as a diagnosis—without confirmatory tests—to bill more. It became common practice for hospitals to admit patients for unrelated medical conditions and then test them throughout their stay to add that diagnosis to the patient's chart, simply to pad the bills.

Of course, if any of those patients later died—for any reason—they were added to the national death count for the Wuhan virus, regardless of whether it was the primary cause of death or even whether the patient had been infected with the virus at all.

Eventually, hospitals grew empty—not just of Wuhan virus patients but of patients in general—and began firing support staff or simply filing for bankruptcy. By mid-2020, a total of forty-two hospitals in the US had closed, primarily due to the elimination of all elective medical care, such as colonoscopies, cardiac surgeries, and cancer treatments.

Of course, many Americans who truly needed medical care were dissuaded by the media from going to a hospital—they had been scared away. Many of my colleagues who work in outpatient surgery centers simply closed their practices. One took a sabbatical to write a book.

Even with corrupt data collection, it became harder and harder to find enough dead people to fuel the ongoing fear pandemic, so the media pivoted and replaced daily death and hospitalization trackers with a new statistical category: "Case Numbers." Most dishonest of all, case numbers reflected nothing but the ongoing expansion of inappropriate testing of healthy people throughout the country, with false positive rates exceeding 80 percent due to inappropriate use of the PCR test.

The widespread public misconception that a positive PCR test in an asymptomatic person indicates the presence of infection has been driving public health care policy in schools, businesses, travel, and even medical treatment centers since early 2020. It is inevitable that by expanding testing to an increasingly large number of people and testing them frequently, "case numbers" will go up—though few if any of these individuals will develop actual symptoms of infection.

In May 2020, the President of Tanzania famously reported having tested a goat and a pawpaw fruit. Both the goat and the pawpaw were positive. Neither developed symptoms. Later that year, billionaire entrepreneur Elon Musk developed cold symptoms and decided to take four tests—same day, same test, same nurse. Two came back positive, and two came back negative. "Something extremely bogus is going on," he said. Musk was right. It would take the CDC until July 21, 2021 to acknowledge that the PCR test is so faulty as to be clinically useless, revoking its emergency use authorization…but prospectively, and not until December 31.

By summer 2021, universal testing—despite being exposed for its complete disconnect from actual illness— continued to be used widely but for a different purpose: to punish the unvaccinated. The new favored statistic became vaccination rates. And as with everything else in the pandemic, the goalposts kept moving.

Initially, Americans were told that the experimental vaccines—approved only under an emergency use authorization—would be necessary to protect the vulnerable, who were mainly old and sick people. This group quickly expanded to include everyone over age sixty-five, regardless of health status. Next came healthy middle-aged adults, then college students, and then teenagers. Forced vaccination of all students down to age twelve, in both public and private schools, is now spreading throughout the country, with public school districts in Los Angeles County leading the way.

This universal vaccination hysteria is being fueled by media that knowingly disseminate propaganda rather than actual news, frequently attacking anyone who points out the known fact that children are simply not affected by this virus in any significant numbers, and that hospitalizations and deaths in children are extremely rare. More children die every year of seasonal flu. With the spread of the new India or Delta variant, there is growing evidence that the experimental vaccine offers little to no protection, whereas natural immunity has now been shown to be essentially 100 percent protective against recurrent infection.

Simply being a child confers near perfect protection as well. In July 2021, Johns Hopkins physician Dr. Marty Makary reviewed over 40,000 cases of infection and all 336 deaths attributed to the Wuhan virus in children and found that not a single healthy child had died from the virus. Despite this, when Florida Governor Ron DeSantis announced that there would be no mask or vaccine mandate for children in his state, he was attacked by local and national news organizations as a callous "anti-science" politician willing to let children die en masse.

From an objective vantage point, Florida has been a tremendous success story. Despite a much older population, Florida's death rate from the Wuhan virus is significantly below that of New York, a state many residents fled from in summer 2020. Where did many of them go? Florida. And while Florida only briefly closed its schools in spring 2020, states like California that kept its schools closed for over a year showed no health benefit to children. In fact, suicide rates in children increased in California between 2019 and 2020.

Rather than reporting on truthful, meaningful discoveries such as the benefits of outpatient treatment, the absence of harm to children from the virus, and the complete protection from all future infection through natural immunity, news organizations chose to disseminate propaganda, revealing that their true intent has been not to provide information but to spread and maintain anxiety and fear throughout the US population.

Women have been particularly emotionally affected by the media's ongoing fear campaign, in large part—as previously discussed—because their husbands have chosen to remain silent rather than challenge the misinformation. This is especially true when the propaganda targets children. Many mothers I speak to in my clinical practice have severely restricted their children's movement for over a year. None of the children have been allowed to attend school due to government-mandated closures, and few have been allowed to play with their friends, even in their own homes.

When asked to explain this paranoid, over-protective, and harmful stifling of their children's social development, the women often justify their behavior by citing "the rise in case numbers" and "the risk of transmitting the virus"—threats they have heard in the news—despite solid evidence that children neither develop serious illness nor transmit the virus to others. Children are more likely to die in a car accident than they are from the Wuhan virus.

This baseless fear appeared to be rampant throughout upper-middle-class liberal households, and it spread within the community like a social contagion. Nearly every day, I speak with parents of patients in my practice who insist that everything they hear in the news, everything they read from their kids' private school administration emails, and everything their neighbors tell them is factual and evidence-based. Their emotions conform with the misinformation they are bombarded with, so few of them have any desire to explore further. My sharing of scientific evidence with them to disprove the delusional thinking has been largely futile, as the combination of media propaganda and social pressure has generated an unstoppable force that drives the hysteria forward.

The phenomenon of social contagion is illustrated clearly in Abigail Shrier's book *Irreversible Damage*, which investigates the explosion of transgenderism among adolescent girls. What had always been an extremely rare event—a girl announcing she was actually a boy—has recently become a common occurrence in junior high and high schools throughout the US. In a permissive environment that encourages "affirmative" receptivity to such transitions, girls download and share videos on social media that legitimize transgenderism as the best explanation for common adolescent angst. One girl comes out as trans, then another, and then another. A transgender club forms at school, and then the girls-turned-boys are invited to choose new names (and pronouns) for themselves. The entire process occurs without the consent or even knowledge of the parents. Before the fall semester ends, up to one-quarter of all girls in a class will have been infected by transgender hysteria. Social contagions are always hysterical because they spread through emotion and peer pressure rather than through sober, considered thinking.

As with the frequently ill-considered decision of young girls to declare themselves boys, the decision of mothers to sequester their children has been not only irrational but harmful, as nearly all of the children in my practice worsened in their symptoms of anxiety and depression by the end of 2020. As a consequence, I was often asked by the mothers to raise their dose of medication or switch to an alternative. My answer of "Let them play freely" was roundly ignored, and some mothers simply terminated treatment to find a new psychiatrist who would reassure them that they were practicing correct mothering by imposing an indefinite period of house arrest on their children.

I experienced the effects of media propaganda and censorship firsthand. After my first major public event in July 2020 in Washington, D.C., where I spoke out against the harm done to all Americans—especially children—by the fear pandemic, I returned to Los Angeles, where I continued to argue that we were being driven to make catastrophic decisions due to fear—largely driven by the corrupt media.

I created a Twitter account, where I exposed the lies and misdirection I saw in the press. My clinical Facebook page, which I had only been using as a passive marketing tool, became an active forum for me to educate an interested public on what actual science was revealing about the pandemic rather than the partisan talking points everyone else was repeating in the media. I also began receiving invitations from churches and civic organizations throughout southern California, where I would speak about the psychological causes and effects of the pandemic, attempting to explain to audiences why we must think for ourselves and act despite our fear rather than because of it. One Orthodox Jewish day school in Beverly Hills had me attend its fall 2020 return-to-school orientation for teachers to reassure them that they and their students would not only be returning to school safely but also that they **must** return to school to prevent further emotional harm.

Wherever I went, I emphasized that given the depth of the lies we are swimming in, my primary directive was to supply truth. My goal was to inform and then encourage everyone to make their own decisions. What I soon discovered was that speaking truth had, in itself, become dangerous. I had made myself a target.

I could never have predicted that urging parents to send their kids to school would provoke an attack against me. *The Epoch Times* produced a one-hour in-studio interview with me over the summer, where I emphasized how destructive school closures had been for children. I posted links to that interview on my social media pages, and it attracted quite a lot of attention. Much of the attention was positive and supportive, but I was struck by several comments from young women who dismissed my arguments as somehow political, biased, and unscientific. I noticed their profile pages contained prominent Leftist slogans and images, as well as photos of animals.

As I began posting more frequently, I saw a curious trend develop: Nearly all my detractors were young, single, white, self-described Democrat women passionate about cats and dogs. Many supported BLM, transgender activism, and other Left-wing causes. All of them hated Donald Trump and equated him with pure evil. They also appeared to be largely unemployed, with considerable free time.

Although I rarely engaged with them and didn't block their accounts or delete their posts, they frequently threatened to report me to the social media authorities for posting "misinformation, lies, and right-wing propaganda." Perhaps I was naïve, but I felt that everyone should have the right to speak freely, especially given how much censorship had already silenced so many.

Slowly but surely, Facebook began attaching "guidance" to my posts. "Partly false" or "Click here for an alternative view" notices appeared whenever I referred to a publication that differed with the official position of either the government, big tech, or mainstream media, which had effectively merged to become one and the same. Any mention of hydroxychloroquine as a viable treatment for the Wuhan virus was immediately flagged. Scientific journal articles showing the lack of efficacy of masks were routinely challenged. Some of my speeches were even removed by YouTube for "spreading misinformation about the pandemic"—exactly as though my ideas and arguments were the equivalent of a contagious disease. All of the data in my speeches were taken from either government publications or peer-reviewed medical journals. But that didn't matter because the findings conflicted with the official narrative. And like an infectious virus, they had to be suppressed and quarantined. I leave it to others to pursue this disturbing analogy.

Eventually, Facebook began censoring my posts. When I uploaded a screenshot of the announcement that my post had been taken down and posted the image to my Facebook page, that post was then censored. I pointed out this irony in the documentary *Seeing 2020*, which covered the medical misinformation and censorship campaign from that year, where sincere evidence-based disagreement was no longer allowed and would, in fact, be punished.

Eventually, I was punished. Florida Governor Ron DeSantis invited me to participate in a roundtable discussion in July 2021, focusing on mask mandates for children in schools. Along with Professor Jay Bhattacharya and others, I argued that there is no scientifically based medical reason to ever place a mask on a child in school. In fact, I declared it to be child abuse. That forum became the basis for the governor's executive order banning mask mandates in Florida schools.

It also led to a Florida state court challenge, numerous Florida-based newspaper articles, and hundreds of messages sent to me by phone, social media, and email from deranged activists convinced that sending a child to school without a mask is equivalent to murder. Many called me a murderer. Many promised to report me to the California Medical Board. One announced, "I know where you live." Twitter suspended my account.

None of the newspapers that covered the story made any attempt to tell the truth, as they sought to distract attention from the mask mandate fight toward a new propaganda campaign—smearing ivermectin, a highly effective and safe medication for use in treating infection from the virus. As many honest physicians have done, I reported the voluminous clinical research showing ivermectin had saved lives. No one is allowed to say this, however. The *Tampa Bay Times* began its article with a quote from an anonymous "medical expert" that read, "Any physician that espouses this should be reported to the state medical association."

It quickly became clear to me that I had been targeted because of my association with Governor DeSantis, universally hated by the Democrat party and the mainstream media, and because I supported the widespread use of a medication that actually worked against the virus. The latter was an especially dangerous position to take, as any treatment that could be shown to be effective was a grave threat to the universal vaccination campaign. Why? The experimental vaccines could only be provided as long as the emergency use authorization (EUA) remained, and the EUA was contingent on there being no acceptable alternative. If ivermectin (or hydroxychloroquine) were to become "acceptable," the vaccine rollout would end.

That is why the media, which are nearly all aligned with the Democrat party that is behind the universal experimental vaccination campaign, uniformly discredit and attack anyone who supports outpatient treatment, as I do. Both have been complicit in both denying Americans access to important information regarding the pandemic and serving as a primary driver of fear.

It is difficult to ignore the immense conflict of interest at the federal level within government agencies that generate health policies. FDA Commissioner Scott Gottlieb joined Pfizer's board of directors in June 2019. Mark McClellan, FDA head from 2002–2004, sits on the board of Johnson & Johnson. Pfizer and Johnson & Johnson both received emergency use authorization from the FDA to bypass standard safety and efficacy testing in bringing its experimental vaccine products to market in early 2020. A FOIA request in June 2020 revealed thousands of pages of emails belonging to Anthony Fauci. Among them, several revealed that he had knowingly funded gain of function research in the Chinese Wuhan Virology Lab, now proven to have been the source of the virus. As Senator Rand Paul has repeatedly pointed out, this makes Fauci directly accountable for the emergency of the viral pandemic, yet Fauci continues to direct national policy on masks and vaccines.

On a more fundamental level, however, government's insistence on the use of emergency orders and executive powers—rather than legislative action—is not only fundamentally at odds with the separation of powers and democratic process. It is a self-aggrandizement of centralized power that serves to strengthen the position of the individuals who exercise that power. Without a fearful citizenry, politicians and unelected government bureaucrats would face unrelenting pressure to relinquish their power to the legislative process. Fear is the fuel that powers the engine of conflict of interest and fosters corruption.

Government health authorities initiated what I consider to be the single greatest act of harm in 2020: closing schools and businesses. This decision was not based on any scientific evidence or rationale, proved entirely ineffective in improving health outcomes, and traumatized the U.S. population. It was driven entirely by one horribly flawed model published by mathematical epidemiologist Neil Ferguson out of the Imperial College London in March 2020 that predicted 2.5 million American deaths from the Wuhan virus. That model was later roundly criticized throughout the world and proved to be off by a factor of ten.

The psychological devastation caused by endless lockdowns continues today, as Americans remain unable to re-integrate into society and continue to show clinically significant symptoms of generalized anxiety, social phobia, and obsessive-compulsive disorder. The most recent reports from the CDC reveal ongoing year-over-year increases in the prevalence of anxiety and depression in the adult population, the largest in those ages eighteen to twenty-nine.

We now know for certain what should have been obvious to government officials from the very beginning—lockdowns don't work. The RAND Corporation reported in September 2021 that not only did lockdowns not save lives, "To the contrary, we find a positive association between shelter-in-place (SIP) policies and excess deaths. We find that following the implementation of SIP policies, excess mortality increases. So, the lockdowns didn't reduce the number of deaths, failed to prevent any excess deaths, and in fact resulted in increased deaths… In other words, lockdowns probably made the situation worse."

Perhaps the greatest tool government has wielded in instigating and maintaining fear is the mask. Despite masks having never been used to prevent the transmission of a respiratory virus, and with no evidence whatsoever to support their use in reducing the spread of the virus, all levels of government instituted mandatory mask mandates throughout the country in summer 2020 and largely maintained them for a full year.

Masks have served no one but those in positions of authority and power. They have only made Americans sicker—physically, emotionally, and psychologically. As early as April 2020, the CDC admitted that mask wearing offered essentially no benefit in preventing the spread of the virus. Their function has been purely symbolic, an emblem of fear, anxiety, and compliance. Even the *New England Journal of Medicine* concurred, describing them as nothing more than "talismans."

Yet as the expectation and acceptance of universal masking (even outdoors) spread throughout nearly every Democrat-controlled urban center in the U.S., liberal women eagerly donned their masks, many transferring their anxiety onto their children by covering up their faces as well. Like cigarettes, masks became an addiction serving to simultaneously reduce and reinforce anxiety. The more time women spent wearing their masks and seeing their children wear masks, the more difficult it became for them to remove them for any significant length of time. One night I saw a young woman riding an electric rental scooter home from a bar she had just left. She did not have a helmet on—but she was wearing her mask.

On August 23, 2021, the governor of Oregon issued a universal outdoor mask order, demanding that anyone over age two wear a mask when outside the home. One week later, on September 1, 2021, the California State Department of Public Health issued "guidance" requiring all K-12 students to wear masks at school. Both orders used as justification the "rise in cases" and the arrival of the "Delta variant" for their remarkable overreach. Despite serving as nothing more than a clove of garlic around the neck, masks came to be seen as an impenetrable shield that would protect against every danger.

When schools closed in the spring of 2020, I marveled at how few mothers protested. I had expected marches in the streets demanding a child's right to an education. In most cases, though, mothers expressed relief that their children would be kept "safe at home," away from the medical risk of contracting the virus by attending school. Despite evidence that children of all ages are actually safer at school than at home, this delusional belief persisted, and fathers did little to counter it. "Of course my kids should be at school," one father reported to me, "but life is hard enough right now with both me and my wife stuck at home—she feels more comfortable with the kids not leaving the house, and I don't want to have to fight with her about it."

Apparently, the advance of government control over all our lives, using "safety" as the sole justification, knows no end. The cancellation of social activities, home sequestration, instituting of masks and hand sanitizer, and now the mad rush for universal vaccination with an experimental biological agent with no safety record but growing evidence of significant physical harm—are all irrational, delusional, psychotic practices born of safetyism. In fact, the experimental Wuhan virus vaccines—made available without FDA approval under an Emergency Use Authorization—are associated with the deaths of more people in the first half of 2021 than all vaccines combined over the previous ten years.

Yet the forced march toward universal vaccination continues. The demand for government control over every aspect of our lives has increased a hundredfold over the past year and a half, driven largely by anxiety and fear. Women, in particular, have been willing agents in this movement because their traditional source of security—men—has largely disappeared. Government has replaced it, in the midst of a pandemic of fear and hysteria, reassuring them that their only hope for safety is to dutifully obey and comply with its orders.

It is a surprising and little appreciated fact that anxiety can be contagious. Post-traumatic stress disorder can be diagnosed in individuals who have experienced trauma indirectly. The *Journal of Anxiety Disorders* reported in 2007 that, following the 9/11 terrorist attacks, "media viewing of tragic events" was sufficient to produce PTSD symptoms in vulnerable populations such as children. When media and government collude to terrorize a population with the goal of making people afraid, even those with no personal experience of physical harm may start to feel injured as well.

Starting in 2020, national media and government health authorities began amplifying fears common in upper-class liberal women that pre-existed the pandemic. They did this by taking advantage of the emotional vulnerability of women lacking strong male support. Rather than report an honest message that we have nothing to be afraid of—that the pandemic nearly exclusively affects the sick and elderly, that healthy people do not spread the disease, and that there are highly effective and safe outpatient treatments available—media and government organizations instead delivered an emotionally charged false narrative that imminent risk of death was lurking everywhere, that no one could be trusted, and that traditional medicine had nothing to offer by way of protection or treatment. What's worse, they shut down all dissenting views, starting at the top with the president of the United States, with no authority to do so whatsoever.

This made-up story confirmed what many women had grown to believe, after decades of indoctrination and propaganda: The world is a dangerous place. Haunted for decades by the suspicion that their fears were irrational, requiring therapy and medication, women now learned that their fears were entirely justified. This explains why so many women have been paradoxically publicly gripped by fear yet privately (in my view at least) relieved that the pandemic exists.

Of course, few women would admit this. Yet it can be inferred indirectly by observing how many women have largely embraced fear-driven, irrational practices such as voluntary house arrest, mask mandates, and universal forced vaccination. Many find it intolerable to witness others—women or men—denying that life itself is unsafe through their display of indifference or even opposition toward these new orders. Today, all that is required to trigger a woman's fear is to show her that the world is actually quite a safe place and that America today is much safer than ever before.

All their lives, American women have been told that their environment—including the men they share it with—cannot be trusted to keep them safe. The arrival of the Wuhan virus could not have been better received by an already traumatized group of Americans. With no one else to turn to, women began to demand that government step in to provide the security—for themselves and their children—that the men in their lives failed to provide.

Leaders at all levels, eager to be seen as "doing something" about the pandemic, were only too happy to comply, closing businesses and schools, ordering all healthy people to place themselves under house arrest, and imposing dehumanizing facial coverings (for both sexes, including children) to a degree not seen under the most repressive Islamic regimes. Government, media, and traumatized women continued their symbiotic relationship that provided all sides with needed support and validation.

Much of the "leadership" from government amounted to nothing more than irrational, incoherent abuse of power. California Governor Gavin Newsom sent California children to Zoom school, forced them to wear masks outdoors at camp, and made it impossible for anyone to eat at a restaurant. He did not feel compelled to follow his own mandates, however, as he dined indoors maskless at the French Laundry restaurant in Napa, joined by the California Medical Association CEO and its top lobbyist. His children continued to attend private school throughout the pandemic, even attending a mask-free camp over the summer.

On the other side of the country in New York, New York City Mayor Bill de Blasio pushed mandatory vaccinations for all, announcing that "the reward of vaccination is freedom." "Tragically," he said, "if you don't get vaccinated, you're going to be left out." Hypocritical and tyrannical politicians rushed to outdo one another, confident that their invocation of emergency power would protect them from legal challenge.

In parallel with the rising demand for government intervention, the heightened state of anxiety has evolved into an impulse to control and be controlled. This makes sense psychologically, as a fearful people always look for a savior that can offer the promise of safety. St. Anthony Fauci has largely served this role for frightened, lost Americans since early 2020. Despite his lack of clinical experience with patients, his financial interests in pharmaceutical corporations, and his frequent flip-flopping on every major position from masks to vaccines, he still maintains his position as chief pandemic policy advisor to the nation. Fauci is the only Director of the National Institute of Allergy and Infectious Diseases to have landed on the cover of *Time*, *People*, and *InStyle* magazine. The timidity of the American people to directly challenge him is only matched by his expansive narcissism. "With all due modesty, I think I'm pretty effective," he said in a July 2020 interview.

Fear also expresses itself in a desire to control others. The best clinical example of this is obsessive-compulsive disorder, an anxiety-based mental illness that expresses itself by a pathological impulse to control one's environment through the performance of rituals that serve no productive purpose other than to temporarily relieve the anxiety. The obsessive-compulsive patient's rigid insistence that these rituals be performed again and again, essentially endlessly, not only tortures the patient but can drive everyone around him to madness.

Since the beginning of the pandemic, many of the most fearful among us have directed their obsessions toward family members, friends, and even strangers in a hopeless yet destructive quest to control the behavior everyone around them. There is a reason the term "Karen," rather than "Peter" or "James," came into popular use in 2020. Women in large numbers—mainly middle-class, liberal white women—took to the streets to accost, shame, and even physically assault anyone out of compliance with their individual views of what constituted virtuous behavior.

In summer of 2020, I was cursed in an elevator for the first time in my life, by a woman, for the crime of entering the elevator without a mask on. The following month, while jogging near my home, a young woman (with a mask on) began screaming at me as I passed her on the sidewalk. A few minutes before that, I had noticed her on another block as she walked in the street wearing headphones, oblivious to the dangers of the passing cars. This time she was standing on the corner, paralyzed from moving, as she waited for a couple to round the corner on the opposite side. Seeing me, she jumped into the street, shaking, and yelled, "Why are you following me—can't you show some respect!" She was hysterical. Meanwhile, those confronted with these outbursts tend to comply, preferring to appease the out-of-control person rather than risk provoking an even more violent outburst. This is how social conformity functions.

These women have targeted their anxiety and fear at others while in public, especially those who choose not to follow the irrational mandates. Until 2020, this behavior was universally condemned. With an entire society paralyzed by fear, and an emasculated male population unwilling to stand up for anyone's security, the number of Karens has exploded throughout liberal urban centers. In both social media and formal news outlets, video and stories of middle- and upper-class white women in coastal cities such as New York, Los Angeles, San Francisco, and Seattle appeared frequently starting in the spring of 2020. Wherever there was a mandate, there was a Karen. Two men were assaulted by a young woman outdoors in Manhattan Beach in August 2020 when she saw them without masks and threw coffee in one man's face. A month earlier, a woman in San Diego emptied a can of mace onto a couple eating hot dogs—maskless—at a dog park. Dozens of these incidents were reported throughout the country in a matter of months, something unimaginable just one year earlier. In effect, Karens became the psychotic enforcers of the arbitrary rules imposed on the population by unelected bureaucrats and unaccountable politicians.

Small businesses were harassed and threatened by local governments throughout the U.S. when their owners refused to comply with nonsensical and arbitrary mandates. Some fought back. In Los Angeles County, Tinhorn Flats bar and grill in Burbank defied the county health order to shut down. In response, Burbank police revoked the business license, arrested the owner three times, and ultimately had the business's electricity turned off. In New Jersey, Atilis Gym was fined $1.2 million for refusing to shut down under the state's business closure mandate. None of these government crusades to crush small businesses benefited the public in any way. Their only function was to punish the holdouts who refused to comply with the government overreach and to set an example for everyone that living in fear is now the only acceptable way to live.

National chains, however, were largely spared and decided to simply tolerate local pressure or government intrusion rather than litigate it in the courts. In fact, they agreed to be the local mandate enforcers. Supermarkets, big box stores, and pharmacies all began to refuse service to customers who dared to shop without a mask on. Countless videos emerged in 2020 from Trader Joe's stores, where small groups of maskless protesters descended on different locations in a display of solidarity against the mask mandate. Without fail, staff refused to ring them up. In Orange County, Mother's Market actually locked a group of maskless customers inside the store, called police, and then had them arrested for trespassing. Even the airline industry followed suit, jumping ahead of the federal government in April 2020, and ordered all passengers into mask compliance. They later lobbied the CDC and FAA to make masks a federal transportation requirement. That requirement went into effect on February 1, 2021, has been extended twice, and shows no sign of ever going away.

Oddly, the argument for a federal mandate for mask-wearing on airlines was that without laws and fines to force everyone to wear a mask, masked passengers would become unruly and disrupt air travel when they saw a passenger without a mask. The result was the exact opposite: In the first six months of 2021, the FAA received 3,000 complaints of unruly passengers, of which over 75 percent involved noncompliance with the federal mask mandate. Airline staff no longer provide alcohol, food, or even beverage service on most flights. Their role has shifted from customer service to mask policing—berating, chastising, and threatening passengers into compliance with medically useless face coverings, even when that means evicting small children and their parents from the aircraft. They now serve only one purpose: to make passengers afraid. Not surprisingly, since 2020, 75 percent of airline cabin crew are female.

With so many powerful institutions aligned against truth and with fear—government, media, corporations—is there any hope for a national recovery? Is the United States doomed to remain in a perpetual state of trauma, its rational decision-making capacity utterly disabled?

There is a way out of this dark pit, but it requires a reformation at every level of society—the individual, the family, and the community. It also requires that new organizations be built. The nation needs an infrastructure that is protected from corruption, one that supports and defends truth rather than the partisan interests of its constituents. All of this will require a recommitment to courage by the remaining Americans who still possess it.

Chapter 4

The Way Forward: Working Our Way Back to Sanity

THE UNITED STATES is now made up of two distinct classes of individuals: the rational and the irrational. Rational individuals are largely fearless, while the irrational tend to be living in tremendous fear. Unfortunately, the rational cannot rescue the irrational. The irrational must first commit to confronting their irrational beliefs and overcoming them. The path forward will be different for each person, but several recurring themes will almost certainly emerge.

For men, it will require a display of courage. They will need to stand up to hysteria and refuse to allow it to drive decision-making. Self-emasculation must end.

For women, it will require emotional restraint. They will need to confront, to the extent they have succumbed to it, the hyper-emotionality that has led them to respond to the current crisis in unhealthy ways.

Finally, to properly address the ongoing damage being done to children, men and women will need to cooperate in this shared endeavor. Children have been victimized by often well-intentioned but thoroughly misguided adults who have abdicated their responsibility to protect their children from harm.

More generally, individual accountability must be found before repair can begin at the group, community, and national levels. Only then can we make full use of organizational and institutional change, which is critical for returning the nation to a state of health for the long term.

When I begin my work with patients, I remind them that everything starts with a shared commitment to reality. The goal of therapy is not to feel good—it is to live in reality, regardless of how it may feel. Over time, patients can modulate the way they feel, but they can never modify reality itself, as it exists independent of them. Attempting to redefine reality is delusional and serves only as a defense against emotional discomfort.

For many women, the threat of mass infection by an invisible pathogen has been terrifying. As previously discussed, women have been primed biologically and culturally to respond to the viral pandemic with uncontained fear, so they cannot be blamed for acting irrationally. Fear activates a primitive protective response that bypasses higher-level thinking. It also inhibits the ability to learn, particularly from one's mistakes.

I suspect that is one reason we have continued to practice self-defeating, ineffectual behaviors such as masking that simply do not achieve the promised outcome of protection. Exploring options that might actually be helpful in reducing the spread of infection or reducing the severity of disease is a process that is simply closed off to us right now—we are not open to it emotionally.

Being afraid, however, does not absolve anyone from the responsibility of taking corrective action. As I have said in my public talks for over a year, "Acknowledge your fear and act in spite of it." I realize that this is not an easy task—especially for women—but it is a necessary one in order to return to a life that is grounded in reality and not emotionality.

I don't mean to imply that feelings are unimportant or that they should be suppressed. That only makes the problem worse. Feelings are meant to be felt. Mistakes are made when feelings are used as the basis for decision-making. One way that fearful women can find immediate comfort and support is by seeking out other women who remain grounded and less susceptible to being infected by fear. Although they are in the minority, those women do exist. Spending time with women, either in-person or through a computer, who reinforce and amplify the fear is simply counterproductive. Although the feeling of validation may provide temporary relief, it does nothing to solve the underlying problem, which is the reliance on groupthink produced by the fear contagion.

A young woman who has been seeing me as a patient for anxiety for several years showed up one day with a mask on her face. I was surprised because her anxiety had been under excellent control for some time. Something had changed. She was living with her mother, who had always been a source of anxiety for her, as well as highly anxious herself. Her mother had become terrified of catching the Wuhan virus and was now wearing a mask everywhere she went. My patient became infected by her mother's fear and began wearing a mask herself to pacify the anxiety they were both feeling. Unfortunately, my patient also spent most of her social time at a park with her mother and her friends, who were also living in fear. She was surrounded by unhealthy emotions.

When I spoke with her, I was quite blunt: I told her to find new friends. To her credit, she did. At her next visit, she showed up smiling and mask-free. "I'm hanging out with a new crowd, and they're not afraid. My mother hasn't gotten any better, but I don't let that bother me much anymore." This new crowd was made up of other young women. All it took for her to lose her fear and begin behaving more rationally was to surround herself with more emotionally healthy women.

Individual therapy can also be helpful in overcoming trauma—and the past two years have certainly been traumatic. One of the most difficult aspects of working with trauma is the repression of feelings. This is different than ordinary fear, which people may consciously avoid dealing with by using distraction, avoidance, or pacification systems like standing six feet apart from one another or wearing a mask. Repression is unconscious. That means you aren't even aware that you are burying your feelings. Becoming aware of what those feelings are and learning to put them into context is the therapeutic objective. This healing process requires a professional therapist, not a friend.

Unfortunately, at least in urban areas, there are few therapists left who offer real therapy. All but a handful of the therapists I used to refer my patients to have either retreated to their homes to pursue remote therapy or simply closed their practices for good and retired. Just as with my physician colleagues, my therapist colleagues have been a profound disappointment to me. Unable to overcome their own fear and irrationality, they have abandoned their profession—and their patients—and refused to offer their professional help in the only setting that truly works for most patients: face-to-face. Many have rationalized their decision to sequester themselves behind a computer screen by arguing that "the patients like it," or that "it's more convenient," but since when is therapy meant to be pleasurable or convenient? Therapy is not massage. It is hard work for both the patient and therapist. Comfort and convenience do not facilitate good therapeutic results. They get in their way.

Group therapy often serves as a useful adjunct to individual therapy, especially when there are many patients all suffering from the same source of pain. For example, Veterans Administration hospitals have been using group therapy for decades to assist veterans with PTSD. There are also groups organized for parents who have lost children. I fully expect a renaissance in group therapy for women who have been traumatized by the viral pandemic and who need to hear the stories of other survivors so that they can find support and learn strategies for coping with overwhelming fear.

Although Alcoholics Anonymous is not group therapy, it can serve as a model for those wishing to overcome addiction. There is a component of addiction that needs to be addressed for many suffering from chronic fear caused by the viral pandemic, so groups that focus on addiction and accountability would be of great value to those addicted to fear.

As with individual therapy, though, most group therapy has been suspended due to the fear pandemic. It will take courageous therapists to restart this important work, along with committed patients willing to challenge their own fears by seeking out real help, rather than the anemic online alternative that has supplanted it.

Women who cannot find any group therapy and have no emotionally grounded female friends will need to look to men to help guide them out of their fear. This places an important responsibility on men to reclaim their masculine authority. Men who have abdicated their leadership role in marriage by failing to set boundaries or challenge their wives when needed must reclaim their position as husband. They must find the courage to confront the women in their lives and remind them that they're safe. They must find a way to say, "We're all going to be OK. I'm here. You need to calm down and let me protect you."

Men have internalized the feminist lie that women don't need them, that women can always take care of themselves, and that offering women security is an insult to their capacity for self-sufficiency. This is hugely destructive for both men and women, and it weakens the social fabric. Men need to provide a counterbalance to the female instinct to minimize risk regardless of the cost. Men need to display, in their words and actions, how it is necessary to venture out of the home, despite the storm, because full engagement with the greater environment is critical to leading a full life.

Risks are everywhere and can never be fully eliminated until death arrives. Focusing on achieving the impossible—a life without risk—guarantees a dead life devoid of joy, excitement, achievement, and growth.

Essentially, men need to show women that fear is a corrosive emotion and an impediment to a healthy life. It is only by taking action **in spite of fear** that one can live a truly free life and achieve one's full potential. Displaying leadership and inspiring confidence requires that a man rediscover his masculinity and act on it in his relationship with women.

American men must no longer tolerate or accept being placed in a feminized role. History shows that it is men and their sacrifices that build our society. They take the most dangerous jobs and assume the most physical risks. They risk their lives mining fuel to heat our homes and going to war to defend our country. They protect women, children, and the elderly through their sacrifice. In the United States, as of 2017, industrial fatality rates for men were ten times higher than those for women. Could it be that successful societies—those that survive over time—are more likely to thrive when men keep women safe?

Many of the traditional male occupational fields such as construction and energy, however, have shed jobs. More men are now working in office settings, sitting for eight hours a day. As the relationship of most men with work becomes less involved with physical labor, and as men's work roles become less traditionally masculine, the role they take in relationships with women becomes more feminine as well. This has led to an imbalance in sex roles and invited the worst impulses of women to predominate in the relationship.

Men are frequently told to control their physical and sexual aggression, but what about women? Are their natures equally flawed, or are they born perfect, with no need to control their natures? When women are allowed or even encouraged to develop hysteria and express uncensored, unrestrained hyper-emotionality, they can wreak havoc on society. Smothering, intrusive, nanny-state behavior can predominate, with an emphasis on a fear-driven obsession for safety and a disregard of the need for intrepid, risk-taking behaviors that display courage.

By normalizing a lack of emotional restraint in women while simultaneously demonizing any expression of healthy aggression in men, American men have been emasculated. This has not only damaged men but also ruined the lives of American women, many of whom will remain alone, unable to find a man who exhibits authentic masculinity to provide a necessary complement to her femininity. A healthy society cannot survive in this way. Men—and women—need to reject this self-destructive path. Men need to start pursuing being men again, stop apologizing, and push back against the fear-driven women—in reality a vocal minority of mostly white liberal affluent women—who are wrecking our world.

Assuming the proper role of husband is of particular importance within a family because of its effect on children. In my practice, I've noticed that emotionally unstable parents have come to use their children to manage their own anxiety at their children's expense. This is destructive and harmful. The children I have seen suffer the most live with mothers consumed by a safety obsession and absent fathers who do not push back against their wives' overzealousness.

The most effective tool I have found to help these children over the past couple of years has been challenging fathers to assert themselves. Once they begin to rationally and firmly address the fears of their wives, the entire atmosphere in the household changes. The children feel safe once again, as they no longer need to take care of the anxiety of their parents. They begin to feel free to take risks, to explore, to play. When I see these children return to my office, there is a noticeable difference. They may still be unhappy and frustrated with the outside world, but they are no longer living lives of fear in their own homes.

So the first step in helping save children from ongoing emotional trauma from the fear pandemic is to cleanse the home environment of fear. It is, unfortunately, not sufficient. This is where the power of the group comes in. For both men and women, spending time with like-minded individuals may make the difference between continual personal growth and an aborted process of self-improvement.

Some of these groups already exist. I recently discovered one in Los Angeles. It meets twice a month in a park to discuss how members are coping with the distressing time they find themselves in. Participants offer support to one another to manage fear, stress, and anxiety. They may offer solutions to the problems they are all facing. When there is no immediate solution, they simply listen. This process incorporates both masculine and feminine qualities—self-assertiveness, courage, vulnerability, and emotional receptivity. It is especially important for fearful yet curious women to join these groups, women open to discarding their fear, so that they can avoid the easy route of grouping themselves together in a way that only amplifies their fear—an echo chamber of Karens. Ideally, the group would be made up of a combination of men and women, so that both sexes can complement one another. Of critical importance is that these meetings be held face-to-face. The full emotional experience of sharing the same space with others cannot be achieved via a web cam. Most Americans have spent a lifetime worth of hours on Zoom in the past eighteen months.

If no local group exists, then you must create one. Telegram and Signal are excellent phone apps that can be used to organize people into a group and share meeting updates. These two apps also have the added benefit of being largely secure from hacking and government spying, inaccessible to the NSA. Members can feel safe in

sharing their names, phone numbers, and email address-
es, as well as their views on controversial subjects. Organized groups committed to truth and rationality generate clarity and courage among their members. They can
be the antidote to isolation as well as the group-think
that pervades the world of social media and the vast majority of so-called news sources. Most importantly, they
serve as building blocks for larger movements that can
change society.

With a group of physicians and one attorney, I
spoke at a church in Los Angeles soon after Los Angeles
County announced that all county employees must be
vaccinated or face termination. A fireman in the audience
raised his hand and asked, "I don't want the vaccine, but
I'm afraid I'll lose my job—what do I do?" My physician
colleague responded, "Start a Telegram group. There
is strength in numbers." He did just that. I received a
message from the pastor a few days later, informing me
that the group the fireman created had already grown
to over 1,000 members. Every one of those members is
a first responder. Just one month later, the *Los Angeles
Times* reported that thousands of first responders have
announced they are refusing the vaccine, and a group
of Los Angeles police officers has filed a lawsuit against
the city, demanding that any officer who has recovered
from infection be made exempt from the vaccine mandate. Groups of like-minded individuals can be powerful
antidotes to fear.

After righting one's family and finding or creating
a local group for individual support and proper model-
ing, it's time to begin organizing for change at a higher level—institutions. The first and most important is
America's schools.

K-12 education has been in decline for several decades. In recent years, the majority of children cannot perform at grade level in math. In my local district of Los Angeles, fewer than half of all eighth-graders performed at grade level in 2019. Graduation rates are abysmal. In the state of Oregon, rather than raise standards, the governor there has eliminated all high school graduation requirements to protect students from the reality of failing.

Perhaps there is a correlation between lowered standards and a dearth of curricula that actually teach reading, writing, and math. With the advent of Zoom school in 2020, parents became aware first-hand of the focus not on the teaching of critical skills but rather the indoctrination pervading both public and private schools. Sexual politics, critical race theory, and revisionist history are now the norm throughout the country. Many teachers are simply professional activists in disguise.

Not only are children's minds being corrupted—their bodies are being invaded as well. In 2020, after a full year and a half of mandatory masking of children, many districts are moving toward mandatory vaccination as a condition of re-enrollment. Private schools have already instituted such policies, despite no scientific evidence supporting a medical benefit, in the presence of significant known and unknown medical risk. If you would like to send your son or daughter in Los Angeles to Brentwood School, Harvard-Westlake, or the Archer School for Girls, admittance is contingent on vaccination.

Public schools have followed, and as soon as the FDA grants full authorization to the now experimental vaccination program, the age threshold will decrease from twelve down to age five. In Los Angeles County, regardless of vaccination status, all children must submit to weekly nasal swab testing and wear masks while indoors. I received a forwarded list of school attendance guidelines from a friend whose children attend school in Northern Virginia. Among other requirements, children at this school are required to wear masks when playing outside, eat lunch six feet part from one another, and enter the school every morning in "socially distanced lines, with masks on." No matter how emotionally healthy a child's parents are, it is not possible to protect any child from pathologic fear and anxiety in this sick and abusive environment. It's time for parents to remove children from the existing school system.

Many are now doing exactly that. Homeschooling is taking off in the United States. Between just 2020 and 2021, the number of homeschooled children in the US nearly doubled from three million to over five million. A rising percentage of parents have announced they will not be re-enrolling their children in the local school this year. They have lost confidence in the ability of the schools to either adequately or properly educate their children and, more recently, have lost faith in the schools to even keep their children safe.

Forcing children to participate in a national experimental drug trial to attend school is a bridge many parents are not willing to cross. Given the power of local and national teachers' unions, who serve only the interests of the teachers and not the children, parent attempts to reform the schools have been largely a failure. What is the alternative? For two-parent households, homeschooling may be the best option. Despite the financial sacrifice, most parents would choose their children's safety and well-being over money. Homeschooling allows parents to select educational materials that provide accurate information, encourage critical thinking, and do not contaminate the student's mind with ideologically driven propaganda on sex, race, history, and even math.

Single parents can also homeschool by joining up with other single parents to share the responsibility of homeschool. Low-cost and even free resources abound, including the growing Prager Resources for Parents and Teachers (PREP) program. If that isn't possible, relocating to an area with a good charter school, where parents have a say in the curriculum and the hiring of teachers, can insulate the children from the largely corrosive atmosphere of government schools. The K-12 public school system, and many private schools, cannot be reformed. A new path to educating America's children is needed.

The American university system is no better. Outside of the STEM fields, virtually no university department in the United States honors academic integrity and discourse. Obsessed with Leftist causes, universities see their mission as indoctrinating their students with ideology rather than teaching humanities and social science. Individual professors who reject this new way are sanctioned, then suspended, and ultimately fired. The most high-profile case in recent years occurred in 2017 at Evergreen College when biology professor Bret Weinstein was forced to resign after challenging a "no whites day" as racist.

The professional graduate schools have fallen as well. Recently a professor of medicine at UCLA made a public apology for referring to women about to give birth as "pregnant women," rather than the now preferred term, "birthing people." Reportedly, several students began crying, and the professor later had to acknowledge that she must have offended them by implying that "only women give birth." Medical doctors are no longer allowed to say that only women give birth, and that there are two sexes. Actual learning is not possible in this environment. Parents should no longer send their children to universities. High school graduates should educate themselves through remote learning or gain work experience in a field that interests them.

If they are able to, an excellent way to spend the first year after high school is living in a foreign country. There are jobs available for Americans to teach English in most countries around the world. These jobs cover all expenses and offer the option of generating savings. More importantly, though, graduates will gain the invaluable experience of life outside the United States, develop an outsider's perspective on their home country, and come to see there are other ways to view and live life. That is what I did immediately after graduating from high school. I spent one year in Geneva, Switzerland. It allowed me to see America's strengths and weaknesses through the eyes of foreigners while "trying on" a different way of life. I returned a year later with a renewed appreciation for my own country and a lifelong curiosity for exploring. Attending an American university today is nothing more than a four-year pampering at an overpriced country club, reinforcing youthful narcissism and breeding disgust toward truth, tradition, and American values in general.

An additional institution that has lost its way is the American medical system, which must be rebuilt from the ground up. Individual physicians have begun to publicly announce they will no longer accept patients who refuse the experimental vaccines. Major hospitals have begun to discriminate against visitors who are unvaccinated, prohibiting them from entering the wards to visit sick family members. This violates the foundation of medical ethics, which demands that all patients be treated equally, regardless of medical status.

When I was trained as a doctor, I was told that whether a patient is a drug addict, an alcoholic, a smoker, or morbidly obese, treatment can never be withheld. As a resident, I frequently treated criminals in the ER who had been injured during the commission of a crime. Often, I felt they didn't deserve treatment, but that was not my decision to make: Every patient must be treated. That ethical model no longer exists. Since 2017, it has no longer been a felony in the state of California to knowingly infect someone with HIV, an incurable chronic illness that is uniformly fatal when not treated. At the same time, healthy people who have no infectious disease at all may now be denied treatment simply for declining an experimental vaccine. The practice of medicine has become largely corrupt.

Although the task of rebuilding America's medical system can only be accomplished through the efforts of doctors, nurses, laboratory technicians, pharmacists, and other healthcare workers, every American can make a contribution to the effort. Is your doctor a coward? Call and ask how he would treat you if you were to catch one of the numerous viral strains of the original Wuhan virus. If the answer is that he would tell you to stay home and wait until you could no longer breathe and then call 911, you should find another doctor. Is your therapist a coward? If you are considering working with one call and ask if they see patients exclusively through Zoom. If they do, then find another therapist. Will your pharmacist fill prescriptions from your doctor without interfering and overriding your doctor's order? If not, then find another pharmacist.

Today, very few doctors, therapists, or pharmacists who are employed by corporations have any freedom to practice as they see fit—they are ordered to follow corporate mandates that have nothing to do with patient care or scientifically sound medical practice. Independent practitioners are the only medical professionals whose primary commitment is to their patient, and many of them still do not educate themselves adequately or display courage when faced with external pressure to conform to politically driven "guidance."

There is a medical apartheid state being built. To preserve medical care for all, a new system that does not discriminate against patients for making informed medical decisions will be the only way forward. Patients have a societal obligation to resist these sinister developments by refusing to support any physician, clinic, or hospital that discriminates against patients for exercising choice in their healthcare decisions.

The research arm of medicine also requires a complete overhaul. An entirely new, independent medical journal system must be developed, along with new professional medical organizations that actually represent their constituents. All the major medical journals, including JAMA, the Lancet, and the NEJM, have disgraced themselves by publishing fraudulent articles to support the pharmaceutical industry and political interests. They can no longer be trusted as reliable sources of information any more than the *New York Times* or CNN. Physicians and scientists will need to build an open-source, peer-reviewed journal system that is not bought or influenced by partisan groups. They will need to restore public confidence in medical research so that "following the science" actually means something other than "following the scientists I agree with."

The professional medical organizations have become partisan political groups that no longer represent physicians and do not concern themselves with the well-being of the patients those physicians treat. The American Medical Association (AMA) has announced that its new policy toward birth certificates is to not include the sex of the baby so as not to influence the baby's "gender development." The American Academy of Pediatrics (AAP) now endorses the chemical castration of children who suffer from gender dysphoria, a mental illness treatable with talk therapy.

I recently received a letter from the AAP, included in a package of sheets of stickers to hand out to children, to encourage all children to drink more water, because "Today, 20% of kids in the United States do not drink water in a given day." Self-sterilization of mentally ill adolescents is not a problem for the AAP, but pediatric hydration is an urgent health crisis. These problems with medical journal and professional organization integrity are not new, but the fall from grace is now complete. They must go. Those in the medical science profession must abandon them as sources of reputable information or professional representation.

The most important reform for the continuing health of our society—medical and psychological as well as political and social—is the guarantee of free expression enshrined in our constitution. Freedom of speech and a free press are essential to a functioning democracy and a free people. There is no example in history of a dictatorship or totalitarian regime that allowed for either. Today, the United States is no longer a free county by these standards. The level of censorship of individual citizens and the press is unprecedented.

Common with all dictatorships, the justification for censorship starts with the announcement of a crisis. In 2020, that crisis was the viral pandemic. That has been the basis for banning speech and publication that questions the crisis or the government response to it in any way. All the social media giants—Facebook, YouTube, Twitter—have admitted without apology that they will not tolerate dissent against current government policy.

Untold harm was done to individuals, society, and to science itself by the decision of media and big tech companies to censor speech that questioned the official view of the proper mitigation and treatment of the virus.

In August 2021, YouTube took down a video interview of United States Senator Rand Paul—a medical doctor—after he questioned the efficacy of using masks to prevent the transmission of respiratory virus, citing actual scientific studies to support his position. Preventing an elected representative of over four million Americans from speaking is not consistent with the values of a free country—it is dictatorship. When ordinary citizens, journalists, and elected officials can no longer count on their privacy rights being respected by the government, or their first amendment rights being honored, we no longer live in a free country.

In order to continue to maintain privacy in our personal communications and to ensure our public speech remains uncensored, we must move to newer, more secure, and more free platforms. For personal communication, I encourage everyone to begin using email providers that guarantee encryption and privacy such as Swiss-based ProtonMail that houses all its servers outside the US. The early private messaging apps, such as WhatsApp, have long abandoned their mission of secure data transmission. Now, those who wish to restrict access to their private communications have the option of apps such as Telegram or Signal. Although no app is completely secure, their independence from the corporate social media giants and their adoption of varying levels of encryption provide a higher degree of confidence for users that what they write and post privately will not be easily accessible to government agencies or the corrupt corporations aligned with them.

I am currently participating in a project to build a decentralized media distribution vehicle that cannot be censored or deplatformed. Designed with the same blockchain technology used by Bitcoin, it promises to be the first of its kind in allowing the producer of the media to fully control content outside the purview of YouTube, Facebook, and Twitter. The project is sponsored by investors who are willing to risk their entire savings to preserve free expression on the internet. What unites the leaders of all these enterprises is not their politics or religion but their commitment to free expression. They understand that a free nation and a free people cannot exist when they cannot speak and write without fear of censorship and cancellation.

All Americans who have chosen freedom over fear should consider abandoning their existing email, social media, and hosting platforms to support systems that value privacy rights and independent communication. There are now options available, and more will emerge if we insist on investing our time and money in supporting them.

Finally, Americans must begin to only support businesses that display courage by rejecting the coercive efforts of politicians and unelected bureaucrats to control the lives of American citizens. If a store insists on discriminating against customers based on health status or personal medical decision-making, refuse to patronize it. Inform the manager that you will take your business elsewhere until the discriminatory policy is ended.

Leaders and officials empowered by societal fear exhibit clear dictatorial tendencies. Mayors and governors gave themselves extraordinary powers during the pandemic and show no signs of being willing to let go of this untrammeled power. Instead, they continue to impose irrational mandates on their citizens without even a pretense of consultation with experts or legislative oversight. Last year, it was masks and "social distancing." This year it is mandatory experimental vaccination. What will it be next year?

The Los Angeles City Council and the LA County Board of Supervisors voted in August 2021 to draft an outright ban on the unvaccinated from all public spaces. Those who refuse to take an experimental vaccine will no longer be allowed to exercise at a gym, dine at a restaurant, or purchase groceries for themselves or their family. Does this sound familiar? The Chinese Communist Party has already begun a social points system that tracks where you go, with whom you speak, and what you say and write. Based on your compliance with government directives and policies, you gain or lose the "right" to work, travel, or attend school. If more Americans do not actively fight back against this direct attack on fundamental liberties, the United States will begin to resemble Communist China more than the country we all grew up in.

The challenge we face starts with the individual, but it ultimately includes organizations and structures that we all rely on to keep our society functioning. As a psychiatrist, I can only treat patients one at a time. There is no prescription that can be written, as there is for a viral infection. Much of the nation has become infected by the pandemic of fear, and there may not be enough treaters to rehabilitate every American. It really is up to the individual to start thinking for himself, or, as Henry David Thorough wrote, "Others will think for you without thinking of you."

That is where we are now—a small group of self-appointed masters giving orders to American citizens too consumed with fear to think for themselves. Will we simply cede our autonomy to a corrupt state that promises to reward the sacrifice of our liberties with eternal security? We can do better. We must do better. We must end the pandemic of fear—before it's too late.

About the Author

Author Photo Credit: Larry Cook

BORN AND RAISED IN LOS ANGELES, Mark McDonald graduated from UC Berkeley before attending medical school at the Medical College of Wisconsin. Trained in both adult and child and adolescent psychiatry at UCLA, he now works primarily with children in private practice in west Los Angeles. Dr. McDonald has lived and worked in Europe, Asia, and Central America. His opinions on topics such as the need to re-open America's schools, and the pandemic of fear in the United States today, have been widely published in local and national news, including the *Wall Street Journal* and *The Federalist.*

References

Introduction

(The Other Pandemic: The Making of a Mass Delusional Psychosis)

CELL PHONE ADDICTION IN ADOLESCENTS

https://www.ncbi.nlm.nih.gov/pmc/articles/PMC6449671/

2019 scholarly review of research on cell phone use in adolescents from around the world and its effect on physical and psychological health. Conclusion: Sleep deficit, anxiety, stress, and depression are all associated with internet abuse and mobile phone usage. Adolescents are highly susceptible to cell phone addiction.

SUICIDE

https://didihirsch.org/media/recent-coverage/l-a-suicide-hotline-sees-rise-in-coronavirus-related-calls-counselors-feel-the-pain/

LA Times, April 4, 2020. Didi Hirsch suicide prevention center director reports hotline received 1,800 calls in March compared to only 20 in February.

SAVING ONE LIFE

https://isi.org/intercollegiate-review/if-it-saves-just-one-life-fallacy/

Exploration of the Andrew Cuomo "If it saves just one life" fallacy.

https://www.nhtsa.gov/press-releases/2020-fatality-data-show-increased-traffic-fatalities-during-pandemic

NHTSA 2020 traffic fatality report: 38,680, the highest since 2007.

DEATH DEMOGRAPHICS

https://www.cdc.gov/coronavirus/2019-ncov/hcp/clinical-care/underlyingconditions.html

May 2021 CDC report on virus death demographics: 80 percent of deaths are in those over age sixty-five, while 1 percent of the population (nursing home patients) represent 35 percent of all deaths.

SAFER AT HOME?

https://www.dailynews.com/2020/04/19/is-los-angeles-countys-safer-at-home-order-necessary-in-its-current-form/

Opinion article, *LA Daily News,* April 18, 2020 challenging LA Mayor Eric Garcetti's "Safer at Home" order.

MADNESS OF CROWDS

https://www.obtaineudaimonia.com/extraordinary-popular-delusions-and-madness-crowds-charles-mackay

Charles Mackay, *Extraordinary Popular Delusions and the Madness of Crowds,* 1841

STUPID BABIES

https://www.theguardian.com/world/2021/aug/12/children-born-during-pandemic-have-lower-iqs-us-study-finds

August 12, 2021, Guardian article reports Brown University department of pediatrics study on IQ of babies born after 2020 show an average drop in IQ of 20 points.

Chapter 1

(The Terrorization of Women:
A Brief Cultural History)

CRIME

https://www.ncjrs.gov/ovc_archives/ncvrw/2017/images/en_artwork/Fact_Sheets/2017NCVRW_UrbanRural_508.pdf

National Center for Victims of Crime (NCVS) 2014 factsheet shows rates of violent crime victimization for men and women equal in urban areas but that women are victimized less in rural and suburban areas.

https://www.statista.com/statistics/423245/us-violent-crime-victims-by-gender/

Statista shows that through 2020, murder victim numbers are evenly distributed among both sexes.

https://bjs.ojp.gov/content/pub/pdf/cv19.pdf

NCVS 2019 survey shows similar rates of violent crime victimization between men and women, urban and rural, compared to 2014. Percentages of men vs. women in category of offender, though, differ by a factor of more than three (75 percent vs. 21 percent men vs. women).

EVOLUTIONARY PSYCHOLOGY

https://psycnet.apa.org/doiLanding?doi=10.1037.2F0022-3514.94.1.168

2008 survey of 17,000 people across 55 cultures shows personality differences between men and women to be universal. Women display higher levels of neuroticism, extraversion, agreeableness, and conscientiousness compared to men.

https://www.bbc.com/future/article/20161011-do-men-and-women-really-have-different-personalities

2016 BBC article reviewing evolutionary psychology research over the past twenty years in the area of male/female personality differences. Conclusion: Men and women are innately different.

THE ROLE OF THE MOTHER

https://www.oxfordclinicalpsych.com/view/10.1093/med:psych/9780190271374.001.0001/med-9780190271374-chapter-39

Donald Winnicott's theory of "primary maternal preoccupation" describes the biological conditioning of postpartum women to develop a powerful identification with her baby, which serves a psychological need for the baby to develop normally.

https://www.scientificamerican.com/article/pregnancy-causes-lasting-changes-in-a-womans-brain/

Scientific American 2016 article shows neural remodeling of a woman's brain following pregnancy that lasts up to two years after a baby's birth.

https://www.sciencedirect.com/science/article/abs/pii/0887618588900047

Community survey of over 18,000 adults shows women have significantly higher prevalence rates of agoraphobia and simple phobia.

https://jamanetwork.com/journals/jamapsychiatry/article-abstract/203838

Generalized anxiety disorder and panic disorder prevalence rates in women are nearly double that of men across cultures, based on examination of 27,000 patients.

https://academic.oup.com/qje/article-abstract/
117/4/1491/1876022 and https://www.nber.org/system/
files/working_papers/w17159/w17159.pdf

Dale and Krueger studies from 2002 and 2011 showing no difference between future earnings of those who attended selective universities and those who were admitted to selective universities but choose to go elsewhere. It is the qualities that led to admission, rather than the college itself, that led to the students' professional success.

WOMEN'S MENTAL HEALTH AND PANDEMIC

https://www.frontiersin.org/articles/10.3389/fgwh.
2020.585938/full (Canada)

The pandemic's effect on mental health has affected women far more than men in the areas of sleep, empathy, and mood disturbances.

https://www.pewresearch.org/fact-tank/2021/03/16/
many-americans-continue-to-experience-mental-health-
difficulties-as-pandemic-enters-second-year/

2020 Pew Research Center report on ongoing psychological damage from pandemic.

https://www.apa.org/monitor/2017/11/numbers

2017 American Psychological Association report on antidepressant use.

Post-WWII Economy and Crime

https://www.history.com/news/post-world-war-ii-boom-
economy

Summarizes the economic surge that followed end of WWII.

https://www.jstor.org/stable/1147382

Describes the rise in crime in 1960s that followed 1940s and 1950s ebb—causes are rapid urbanization and industrialization and changes in demographic structure.

1970S AND THE RISE OF ENVIRONMENTALISM

https://www.bbc.com/future/article/20200420-earth-day-2020-how-an-environmental-movement-was-born

BBC describes the history of the birth of the environmental movement in the US.

https://www.theguardian.com/lifeandstyle/2019/mar/12/birthstrikers-meet-the-women-who-refuse-to-have-children-until-climate-change-ends

BirthStrikers: Women are refusing to have children "until climate change ends."

https://www.ncbi.nlm.nih.gov/pmc/articles/PMC4246304/

Fertility reduction will not improve the environment.

https://www.independent.co.uk/life-style/health-and-families/greta-thunberg-aspergers-eating-disorder-malena-ernman-interview-a935520html

Greta Thunburg's mental illness of OCD and eating disorder drive her activism and neuroticism.

https://www.nydailynews.com/opinion/ny-oped-sorry-greta-youre-mostly-wrong-20190924-t7depfksqnfmhpjgcwv6iyfesm-story.html

Why Thunburg is wrong on the science.

https://thehill.com/policy/energy-environment/426353-ocasio-cortez-the-world-will-end-in-12-years-if-we-dont-address

AOC declares the world will end in twelve years if we don't address climate change.

https://newrepublic.com/article/154879/misogyny-climate-deniers

Climate activist criticism linked to misogyny.

RELIGIOUS RIGHT, ABORTION, AND MISOGYNY

https://letsbreakthrough.org/anti-abortion-misogyny-its-never-about-the-children/

Opposition to abortion by men equates to hatred of women...misogyny.

https://www.jstor.org/stable/3177522

ANTIABORTION, ANTIFEMINISM, AND THE RISE OF THE NEW RIGHT.

https://www.rollingstone.com/tv/tv-features/handmaids-tale-season-4-moss-atwood-interview-1166738/

2021 *Rolling Stone* article describes Trump, the Handmaid's Tale, and political activism by Planned Parenthood.

https://abcnews.go.com/Politics/handmaids-tale-protesters-target-kavanaugh/story?id=57592706

Brett Kavanaugh and the 2018 hearing...Handmaid's Tale protest.

9/11 AND AMERICAN IMPERIALISM

https://www.e-ir.info/2012/08/14/post-911-us-foreign-policy-continuation-of-new-imperialist-ambitions/

https://books.google.com/books?id=Crs1bGcjAp8C&printsec=front_cover

Argues that 9/11 attack was a direct result of US imperialism.

https://www.ncbi.nlm.nih.gov/pmc/articles/PMC2697567/

https://journals.sagepub.com/doi/full/10.1177/2378023119856825

Women report being especially fearful of future terrorist attacks after 9/11.

RACISM

https://www.justice.gov/hatecrimes/hate-crime-statistics#piechart

Department of Justice 2019 FBI hate crime report tables, charts, graphs that show decrease from 2018 in reported number of racially motivated hate crimes.

https://apnews.com/article/hate-crimes-rise-FBI-data-ebbcadca8458aba96575da905650120d

AP News report from November 2020 shows overall hate crimes up but racial hate crimes down, including for black victims.

https://www.adl.org/media/15335/download

Anti-Defamation League table of FBI hate crime statistics from 2000–2019, categorized by race, religion, etc.

https://www.uber.com/newsroom/being-an-anti-racist-company/

Uber's anti-racist policies explained.

https://www.cdc.gov/healthequity/racism-disparities/director-commentary.html

CDC states racism is a serious threat to public health.

https://time.com/3929917/obama-n-word-marc-maron-podcast-interview/

Obama says racism is "still part of our DNA."

https://www.theguardian.com/us-news/live/2021/jun/01/joe-biden-tulsa-oklahoma-race-massacre-us-politics-live

Biden announces white supremacists to be most lethal terrorist threat to the US today.

GUN CRIME AND MASS SHOOTINGS

More Guns, Less Crime: Understanding Crime and Gun Control Laws. John Lott. 1998.

The War on Guns: Arming Yourself Against Gun Control Lies. John Lott 2016.

Gun Control Myths: How Politicians, the Media, and Botched "Studies" Have Twisted the Facts on Gun Control. John Lott. 2020.

Lott conducts an exhaustive review of national FBI crime statistics, as well as state-by-state data on crime and gun ownership, to authoritatively reject the argument that legally owned guns substantially contribute to crime, and that eliminating them and enacting "safe spaces" saves lives and improves public safety. He also pulls apart the lie that mass shootings are on the rise in the US and that restricting gun sales will decrease their frequency.

ANXIETY PREVALENCE IN AMERICAN WOMEN

https://www.nimh.nih.gov/health/statistics/any-anxiety-disorder

Anxiety disorder prevalence in Americans, both in general and for women in particular.

https://www.huffpost.com/entry/women-and-prescription-drug-use_n_1098023

Women and prescription drug use: 2010–2011.

https://www.theguardian.com/commentisfree/cifamerica/2011/nov/21/one-in-four-women-psych-meds

The Guardian asks in 2011, "Are women crazy?"

https://www.statista.com/statistics/1133682/antianxiety-medication-use-by-age-gender-us/

Women and anti-anxiety prescriptions: 2019.

https://adaa.org/find-help/treatment-help/medication-options

Historical prevalence of anti-anxiety medication in the US.

https://www.cdc.gov/nchs/data/hus/2016/080.pdf

CDC data from 1998–2014 shows prevalence of anti-anxiety prescription drug use by age and sex.

Eating Disorder Prevalence in American Women

https://academic.oup.com/ajcn/article/109/5/1402/5480601

American Journal of Clinical Nutrition review of prevalence of eating disorders in women, showing a doubling of prevalence in most continents throughout the world, including North America.

Traditional Gender Roles in Male / Female Relationships

https://www.deseret.com/2019/5/20/20673829/which-is-better-for-families-traditional-religious-gender-roles-or-secular-ones

Judeo-Christian couples prefer traditional male / female gender roles.

Chapter 2
(Dereliction of Duty:
How Feminized American Men Failed Their Women)

FAILURE TO LAUNCH

https://www.scientificamerican.com/article/failure-to-launch-syndrome/

Scientific American article notes the rise of home-dwelling men age 25–54 who live in their parents' basements, not working, with no desire to work. One reason: Safety.

https://www.phillymag.com/news/2012/02/20/the-sorry-lives-and-confusing-times-of-today-s-young-men/

2012 Philadelphia City Life Article notes men don't have jobs, are dropping out of college, play video games all day, and watch porn all night. Sperm counts are low. "Why won't guys grow up?"

https://www.jaacap.org/article/S0890-8567(15)00729-7/fulltext#relatedArticles

JAACAP article on failure to launch, written in 2017, describes "young adults overwhelmed by the demands of adulthood."

https://www.forbes.com/sites/neilhowe/2017/10/02/youre-not-the-man-your-father-was/?sh=52c2cd8d8b7f

Forbes article written by Neil Howe in 2017 describes the decline in masculinity among America's men.

TESTOSTERONE LEVELS IN MEN

https://academic.oup.com/jcem/article/92/1/196/2598434

JCEM (Journal of Clinical and Endocrinology & Metabolism) reports in 2007 a decades-long decline in testosterone levels in men amounting to approximately 1 percent per year since 1987. The declines noted were independent of age.

https://jamanetwork.com/journals/jama/article-abstract/2612615

JAMA 2017 investigation report substantial increase in supplemental testosterone use in American men from 2000 to 2013.

Decline in Physical Strength in American Men

https://www.jhandtherapy.org/article/S0894-1130(15)00212-4/fulltext

2016 Journal of Hand Therapy study shows drop in grip strength in millennials—male and female—compared to same-age cohorts from previous decades. Grip strength force declined in men from 117 pounds in 1985 to 98 pounds in 2016 for men in the 20–34-year-old group.

MASCULINITY

https://www.pewresearch.org/fact-tank/2019/01/23/americans-views-on-masculinity-differ-by-party-gender-and-race/

2019 Pew Research poll on views of masculinity finds only 31 percent of American men of all races view themselves as "very masculine," with white men at 28 percent. Political split: 39 percent of Republican men vs. 23 percent of Democrat men view themselves as very masculine. Among Republicans, 78 percent view valuing masculinity as a good thing, compared with only 49 percent of Democrats.

https://www.pewresearch.org/social-trends/2017/12/05/ on-gender-differences-no-consensus-on-nature-vs-nurture/

2017 Pew Research poll finds that college-educated men see themselves as less masculine than those with less education. Younger women (millennials) do not see themselves as feminine (19 percent), compared to 36 percent of boomers.

WOMEN IN MEDICINE

https://www.aamc.org/news-insights/press-releases/majority -us-medical-students-are-women-new-data-show

More than half of all US medical students are now women.

WOMEN IN THE WORKFORCE

https://www.nber.org/system/files/working_papers/ w23371/w23371.pdf

National Bureau of Economic Research 2017 finding that wage stagnation for men parallels increase in women entering workforce.

EGALITARIANISM, HOUSEWORK, AND SEXUAL FREQUENCY IN MARRIAGE

https://www.asanet.org/sites/default/files/savvy/journals/ ASR/Feb13ASRFeature.pdf

American Sociological Review 2012 publication finds that both husbands and wives in couples with more traditional housework arrangements report higher sexual frequency, suggesting the importance of gender display rather than marital exchange for sex between heterosexual married partners.

Part-time / Full-time work: Psychological Effects on Mothers

https://psycnet.apa.org/doiLanding?doi=10.1037%2Fa0025993

Journal of Family Psychology reports psychological benefit of part-time work for mothers, their children, and their family.

https://www.census.gov/library/stories/2020/05/the-choices-working-mothers-make.html

2018 US Census report on percentage of full-time vs. part-time working mothers.

https://hbr.org/2017/05/does-a-womans-high-status-career-hurt-her-marriage-not-if-her-husband-does-the-laundry

Harvard Business Review 2017 research publication reveals that wives who believed that they held higher status positions than their husbands were more likely to experience feelings of resentfulness or embarrassment, which in turn had a negative effect on marital satisfaction and increased the likelihood they were thinking of divorce.

https://academic.oup.com/qje/article-abstract/130/2/571/2330321?redirectedFrom=fulltext#173450329

Quarterly Journal of Economics 2015 publication examines consequences of income differences in households. "In couples where the wife earns more than the husband, the wife spends more time on household chores; moreover, those couples are less satisfied with their marriage and are more likely to divorce."

Actual publication here: https://pubsonline.informs.org/doi/abs/10.1287/orsc.2017.1120.

https://www.asanet.org/press-center/press-releases/women -more-likely-men-initiate-divorces-not-non-marital-breakups

2015 American Sociological Association report notes that 69 percent of all divorces are initiated by women between 2009–2015.

**https://www.themodernman.com/blog/are-college-educated
-women-bad-wife-material.html**

Article cites study published in the American Law and
Economics Review showing that among college-educated couples, 90 percent of divorces are initiated by women.

TOXIC MASCULINITY

**https://www.apa.org/pi/about/newsletter/2018/09/
harmful-masculinity**

American Psychological Association 2018 report ties
masculinity to violence.

RAPE CULTURE

https://www.marshall.edu/wcenter/sexual-assault/rape-culture/

What does "rape culture" mean?

**https://ucr.fbi.gov/crime-in-the-u.s/2019/crime-in-the-u.s.-
2019/tables/table-15**

FBI 2019 national crime statistics report.

**https://ucr.fbi.gov/crime-in-the-u.s/2019/crime-in-the-u.s.-
2019/topic-pages/rape.pdf**

FBI 2013 redefining of rape in collecting national crime
statistics.

**https://www.aau.edu/newsroom/press-releases/aau-releases-
2019-survey-sexual-assault-and-misconduct**

Association of American Universities 2019 survey of sexual assault.

https://www.aau.edu/sites/default/files/AAU-Files/Key-Issues/Campus-Safety/Revised%20Aggregate%20report%20%20and%20appendices%201-7_(01-16-2020_FINAL).pdf

Association of American Universities 2020 survey of sexual assault.

https://www.bjs.gov/content/pub/pdf/fvsv9410.pdf

US Department of Justice 2016 Special Report on Female Victims of Sexual Violence 1994–2010.

https://www.bjs.gov/content/pub/pdf/vvcs02.pdf

US Department of Justice 2005 National Crime Victimization Survey for college students 1995–2002.

Feminist Ideology and its Toxic Effect on Male-Female Relationships

The Flip Side of Feminism by Suzanne Venker and Phyllis Schlafly, 2011.

False statistics—Infection, Hospitalization, and Death Rates from the Wuhan Virus.

https://www.cdc.gov/nchs/nvss/vsrr/covid_weekly/index.htm?fbclid=IwAR3-wrg3tTKK5-9tOHPGAHWFVO3Dfsl kJ0KsDEPQpWmPbKtp6EsoVV2Qs1Q

CDC reports only 6 percent of all Wuhan virus deaths reported occurred in health people. 94 percent of all deaths included additional comorbidities, with on average 2.6 additional causes of death.

https://nbc25news.com/news/local/cdc-94-of-covid-19-deaths-had-underlying-medical-conditions

NBC News report on CDC findings that only 6 percent of Wuhan virus deaths occurred in healthy people.

https://www.usatoday.com/story/news/factcheck/2020
/04/24/fact-check-medicare-hospitals-paid-more-covid-19-
patients-coronavirus/3000638001/

USA Today confirms claim that hospitals reimbursed substantially more by federal government when listing "COVID-19" on the list of diagnoses.

https://www.theepochtimes.com/cycle-threshold-value-
missing-in-ccp-virus-case-numbers-experts_3540881.html
?utm_source=news&utm_medium=email&utm_
campaign=breaking-2020-10-21-3&fbclid=IwAR1eFhr
19pN465qtGl8XORGKlEposkJxw0E5k2k1x0fDu
flUvg3I03VaeiQ

CDC's PCR test cycle rates lead to elevated false positive case numbers.

CHILDREN AND THE VIRUS

https://news.yahoo.com/german-study-shows-low-
coronavirus-133206550.html

July 2020 German school study finds children do not spread disease and actually act as a "brake on infection."

https://www.cdc.gov/mmwr/volumes/70/wr/
pdfs/mm7024e1-H.pdf?fbclid=IwAR153webZW
liXPJyr0SUM7QGKV2J-5XoFpwVfvmNBZC2Lvi6NyIB
ya6uTBM

CDC reports 30 percent increase in youth suicide attempts in 2020 compared with prior year.

https://www.wsj.com/articles/pandemic-toll-children-
mental-health-covid-school-11617969003?fbclid=
IwAR2yEHsCvsS8F7VQTjGd7UdbFNZwpL80hx1
qGdL3S-mjbm_LEuooB5epz8A

Wall Street Journal on the pandemic of social isolation, stress, and mental-health issues facing children after one year of school closures.

https://www.pe.com/2021/03/30/southern-california-suicides-down-during-coronavirus-pandemic-but-not-among-young-people/?utm_email=E44D9493A4BD7421C57244AB74&g2i_eui=l1hHBZmxw9%2F3BUTOPT%2B8ItN%2BinSLPkLj&g2i_source=newsletter&utm_source=listrak&utm_medium=email&utm_term=Read%20more&utm_campaign=scng-ivdb-localist&utm_content=curated&fbclid=IwAR0ok8GLiXYapcV6wYmdz26EK_t-nF3O15_zrVgua8sYrxTCFlpPeEPq1wU

Three out of four Southern California counties report suicides rose in youth in 2020.

https://www.cdc.gov/mmwr/volumes/69/wr/pdfs/mm6932a1-H.pdf?fbclid=IwAR2vz7tBo1B2zmrsk2LyDqoI07OZk7NwiDSyocZPgZuJIsAoYAgTiIDbjHY

CDC report from June 2020 reveals 300 percent increase in incidence of anxiety and 400 percent increase in incidence of depression in youth compared to same period last year.

Chapter 3

(Fanning the Flames: The Role of Media and Government)

https://thefederalist.com/2020/10/12/cdc-study-finds-overwhelming-majority-of-people-getting-coronavirus-wore-masks/?fbclid=IwAR1j81e7lhGi15T1Q2ImbMmH2QvdZ6-dsc8xnAdJjnUa9_iwIyMw5lw_Ics

CDC reports findings of its own study on masks showing they offer no value in preventing spread of Wuhan virus: "In the 14 days before illness onset, 71 percent of case-patients and 74 percent of control participants reported always using cloth face coverings or other mask types when in public."

https://www.cdc.gov/nchs/nvss/vsrr/covid_weekly/index.htm#Comorbidities

CDC reports 95 percent of all virus deaths included additional causes of death, nearly three on average, throughout the pandemic.

https://wpde.com/news/nation-world/man-who-died-in-motorcycle-crash-counted-as-covid-19-death-in-florida-report-07-18-2020

July 2020 Florida motorcycle death attributed to virus.

https://www.mprnews.org/story/2020/04/03/change-to-death-certificates-could-boost-covid19-counts

Minnesota state changes cause of death criteria for all pneumonia patients to presumed Wuhan virus without confirmatory testing.

https://www.hfma.org/topics/news/2020/04/increased-medicare-payments-for-covid-19-care-to-stretch-back-to.html

Medicare offering hospitals bonuses for "Covid diagnosis" and up to an additional $35,000 to put patients with that diagnosis on a ventilator.

https://www.beckershospitalreview.com/finance/42-hospitals-closed-filed-for-bankruptcy-this-year.html

June 2020 Becker's Hospital Review reports 42 hospitals filed for bankruptcy so far that year.

https://www.reuters.com/video/watch/idOVCCIUZCJ

In May 2020, Tanzanian President John Magufuli tests a goat and a pawpaw—both returned positive results.

https://www.washingtonpost.com/nation/2020/11/13/elon-musk-covid-test-bogus/

In November 2020, Elon Musk reports he took four PCR tests after experiencing cold symptoms: Two came back positive and two came back negative.

https://www.cdc.gov/csels/dls/locs/2021/07-21-2021-lab-alert-Changes_CDC_RT-PCR_SARS-CoV-2_Testing_1.html

On July 21, 2021, CDC announces it will revoke emergency use authorization for the PCR test—on December 31, 2021.

https://www.wsj.com/articles/cdc-covid-19-coronavirus-vaccine-side-effects-hospitalization-kids-11626706868?mod=searchresults_pos3&page=1

Dr. Marty Makary reports on July 19, 2021 having personally reviewed over 40,000 cases of infection and 335 deaths in children attributed to the Wuhan virus and found that not a single healthy child died.

https://www.pe.com/2021/03/30/southern-california-suicides-down-during-coronavirus-pandemic-but-not-among-young-people/

Youth suicides increase in California between 2019 and 2020.

https://www.medrxiv.org/content/10.1101/2021.08.24.21262415v1

August 2021 Israeli study shows natural immunity far superior to vaccine to prevent reinfection.

https://www.science.org/news/2021/08/grim-warning-israel-vaccination-blunts-does-not-defeat-delta

August 2020 *Science* article shows 60–80 percent of hospitalized Israelis previously infected, despite nearly 60 percent vaccination rate.

https://www.nejm.org/doi/full/10.1056/nejmp2006372

New England Journal of Medicine concludes masks serve as little more than "talismans" against anxiety.

https://pubmed.ncbi.nlm.nih.gov/33289900/

IFR (Infection Fatality Rate) of Wuhan virus, by age, compared with other causes of death, reveals car accidents kill more people under age 34.

https://www.cdc.gov/mmwr/volumes/70/wr/mm7013e2.htm

CDC study from 8/20–2/21 shows significant increase in anxiety and depression prevalence in US population, with greatest increase in age 18–29.

https://www.cdc.gov/mmwr/volumes/69/wr/mm6945a3.htm

CDC study from January 2, 2020 to October 17, 2020 shows increase by one-third in incidence of ER visits for children for psychiatric emergencies.

SOCIAL CONTAGION

Irreversible Damage by Abigail Schrier covers the recent transgender craze sweeping the nation.

GOVERNMENT CONFLICT OF INTEREST

https://www.businessinsider.com/scott-gottlieb-goes-from-fda-commissioner-to-pfizer-board-member-2019-6

June 28, 2019 *Business Insider* reports FDA head leaves FDA to join Pfizer's board of directors. Mark McClellan, FDA head from 2002–2004, sits on the board of Johnson & Johnson.

https://nypost.com/2021/06/03/fauci-emails-heres-what-we-learned/

June 3, 2021 *New York Post* articles discusses Fauci email release from FOIA request.

https://www.foxla.com/news/california-governors-office-says-to-put-on-mask-between-bites

October 8, 2020: Newsom's office encourages Californians, "Don't forget to keep your mask on in between bites."

https://www.washingtontimes.com/news/2021/aug/26/democrats-party-of-tyrants-reward-of-vaccination-i/

August 26, 2021, Bill de Blasio orders all New Yorkers to be vaccinated in order to maintain their freedom.

https://www.nature.com/articles/d41586-020-01003-6

Imperial College London's Neil Ferguson's March 2020 publication of model that predicted 2.2 million deaths from the Wuhan virus in the US.

https://www.nber.org/system/files/working_papers/w28930/w28930.pdf

RAND Corporation study finds government lockdowns did not save lives. The RAND/USC team is unsparingly direct: "[W]e fail to find that shelter-in-place (SIP) policies saved lives. To the contrary, we find a positive association between SIP policies and excess deaths. We find that following the implementation of SIP policies, excess mortality increases. So, the lockdowns didn't reduce the number of deaths, failed to prevent any excess deaths, and in fact resulted in increased deaths. Additionally, countries that locked their citizens in their homes were experiencing declining—not increasing—excess mortality prior to lockdowns. In other words, lockdowns probably made the situation worse."

https://www.oregon.gov/newsroom/Pages/NewsDetail.aspx?newsid=64307

On August 24, 2021, Governor Kate Brown of Oregon issues universal outdoor mask mandate.

**https://www.cdph.ca.gov/Programs/CID/DCDC/Pages/
COVID-19/K-12-Guidance-2021-22-School-Year.aspx**

On September 1, 2021, California Department of Public
Health issues school "guidance" requiring all students to wear
masks at school.

https://vaers.hhs.gov

Vaccine Adverse Events Reporting System confirms
5,718 deaths from the Wuhan virus vaccines through the end
of June 2021.

**https://www.cdc.gov/coronavirus/2019-ncov/vaccines/
safety/adverse-events.html**

CDC reports Wuhan virus vaccines "safe and effective."

<u>PTSD</u>

**https://www.psychiatry.org/patients-families/ptsd/what-is-
ptsd**

American Psychiatric Association clinical criteria for PTSD.

https://pubmed.ncbi.nlm.nih.gov/17276653/

Journal of Anxiety Disorders 2007 publication finds exposure to "media-based traumatic images" or "media viewing
of tragic events" following 9/11 terrorist attacks is sufficient
to produce PTSD symptoms in vulnerable populations such
as children.

**https://www.scientificamerican.com/article/post-traumatic
-stress-disorder-can-be-contagious/**

Scientific American article explains how PTSD can be
contagious.

https://www.instyle.com/news/dr-fauci-says-with-all-due-modesty-i-think-im-pretty-effective

July 2020 *In Style* magazine interviews Anthony Fauci and features him on its cover. "With all due modesty, I think I'm pretty effective."

https://pubmed.ncbi.nlm.nih.gov/18436429/

How OCD can be used as a template in understanding how anxiety leads to a desire to control one's environment.

https://www.foxla.com/news/bloody-brawl-breaks-out-after-woman-throws-coffee-in-mans-face-for-not-wearing-mask

In August 2020, a Manhattan beach woman throws coffee in man's face outdoors because he is not wearing a mask.

https://nypost.com/2020/07/26/woman-maces-couple-for-not-wearing-masks-at-california-dog-park-video/

A Woman in San Diego empties a can of mace on a maskless couple eating hot dogs outside at a dog park.

https://www.latimes.com/california/story/2021-04-09/burbank-restaurant-repeatedly-defies-covid-closure-orders

Tinhorn Flats bar and grill in Burbank refuses to close in violation of LA County health order. The owner is arrested three times, his business license is revoked, and power to the business is shut off.

https://nypost.com/2020/12/14/nj-gym-that-defied-covid-19-lockdown-fined-more-than-1-2m/

Atilis Gym in New Jersey is fined $1.2 million for refusing to close under lockdown orders.

Chapter 4
(The Way Forward:
Working Our Way Back to Sanity)

OVERCOMING FEAR THROUGH GROUPS

https://www.latimes.com/california/story/2021-09-13/vaccine-exemption-requests

On September 13, 2021, thousands of LAPD officers promise to file exemption requests for medical or religious reasons to bypass vaccine mandate.

https://www.theepochtimes.com/mkt_app/los-angeles-county-to-mandate-covid-19-vaccine-passports-officials_3999372.html?utm_source=appan2028170?v=ul

On September 13, 2021, LA County Health Department Director Barbara Ferrer mandates ban on access to bars and clubs for the unvaccinated. Next step—restaurants.

AIRLINES

https://www.faa.gov/news/press_releases/news_story.cfm?newsId=26200

FAA reports on June 14, 2021 that it has been levying fines of up to $15,000 against passengers who refuse to wear masks while flying and that of the 3,000 reports of unruly passengers filed since January 1, over 75 percent involved passengers refusing to comply with the federal mask mandate.

https://datausa.io/profile/soc/flight-attendants

75 percent of airline cabin crew are female.

Failure of the American Education System and the Home-Schooling Alternative

**https://www.pewresearch.org/fact-tank/2017/02/15/
u-s-students-internationally-math-science/**

2017 Pew Research Center report on American students
falling behind in math, science, and reading compared to other industrialized nations.

**https://nces.ed.gov/nationsreportcard/subject/publications/
dst2019/pdf/2020015XL8.pdf**

National Center for Education Statistics 2019 report on
Los Angeles eighth-graders shows fewer than half meet the
minimum proficiency level for math.

**https://www.washingtonexaminer.com/news/oregon-
bill-ending-reading-and-arithmetic-requirements-
before-graduation**

Oregon governor ends all high school graduation
requirements.

**https://www.census.gov/library/stories/2021/03/home
schooling-on-the-rise-during-covid-19-pandemic.html**

March 2021 US Census Pulse Survey shows increase
in numbers of homeschooled children from three million in
2020 to over five million in 2021.

**https://www.wsj.com/articles/california-leftists-try-to-
cancel-math-class-11621355858**

The WSJ journal explains what "racist math" is on May
18, 2021.

https://www.prageru.com/kids/

PREP program for kids to assist parents who homeschool
their children.

**https://thefederalist.com/2020/07/01/3-years-ago-bret-
weinstein-endured-the-precursor-to-todays-riots/**

Biology professor Bret Weinstein's firing by Evergreen
College for challenging "no-whites day" on campus as racist.

CORRUPTION IN THE US HEALTH CARE SYSTEM

https://bariweiss.substack.com/p/med-schools-are-now-denying-biological

July 27, 2021 report by Bari Weiss on Substack on UCLA professor of medicine apologizing to medical students for using the term "pregnant woman," as that implies "that only women give birth."

https://apps.uclahealth.org/e/es?s=1108064982&e=74992&elqTrackId=af5a6f047aa64eb69c1633ddd78d6e68&elq=39901d73b9d7454bba67a571d15cd48e&elqaid=266&elqat=1

UCLA refusing access to hospitals and clinics for unvaccinated visitors.

https://www.cnn.com/2017/10/07/health/california-hiv-bill-signed/index.html

2017 California governor Jerry Brown reduces from felony to misdemeanor crime of knowingly infecting someone with HIV.

CORRUPTION IN THE US FINANCIAL SYSTEM

https://www.nytimes.com/2021/01/11/us/politics/trump-politicians-donations-degrees.html

January 2020 *NYT* article describes how financial institutions are cutting ties with President Trump under pretext he led an "insurrection" at the US Capitol.

https://www.foxbusiness.com/politics/republicans-banking-access-bill-woke-cancel-culture

Fair Access to Banking Act March 2020 seeks to block "woke banking" discrimination.

https://thebl.com/us-news/gofundme-cancels-grieving-fathers-fundraiser-for-son-who-died-from-vaccine.html

On September 10, 2021, GoFundMe cancels fundraiser of father whose son died from vaccine.

https://foreignpolicy.com/2021/07/23/economists-warn-inflation-70s-biden-nixon/

Inflation under President Biden heading toward a 1970s out-of-control spiral.

https://www.cnn.com/2021/05/25/business/inflation-economic-growth-biden/index.html

Even CNN agrees inflation under President Biden is a problem.

https://apnews.com/article/joe-biden-health-coronavirus-pandemic-us-supreme-court-8d397f378c01c369f0d86 18a4d9b3a83

Biden administration cancels legal right of property owners to collect rent or evict tenants for failure to pay.

CRYPTOCURRENCY

https://coinmarketcap.com

Source of cryptocurrency market capitalization tracked daily.

https://www.wsj.com/articles/bitcoin-comes-to-el-salvador-first-country-to-adopt-crypto-as-national-currency-11631005200

On September 7, 2021, El Salvador became the first country to adopt BitCoin as a national currency.

https://time.com/nextadvisor/credit-cards/credit-cards-with-crypto-rewards/

Credit cards offering rewards in BitCoin.

Why Alternative Media are Needed

https://www.paul.senate.gov/news/dr-rand-paul-blasts-youtube-continued-censorship

Senator Rand Paul's August 10, 2021 press release describing YouTube censorship of his video interview questioning the efficacy of masks in preventing the transmission of respiratory virus.

https://www.wsj.com/articles/tucker-carlsons-spying-allegations-being-investigated-by-national-security-agency-watchdog-11628607609

NSA investigating itself after admitting it illegally surveilled Fox News host Tucker Carlson's personal phone and email communications.

https://thehill.com/policy/technology/517023-lawsuit-accuses-facebook-of-spying-on-instagram-users-with-mobile-phone

Facebook sued over Instagram spying on users.

https://www.businessinsider.com/parler-election-conservative-social-media-app-stop-the-steal-2020-11

Parler app soars to most downloaded app—1 million users per day.

MOVEMENT TOWARD TOTALITARIANISM

https://www.latimes.com/california/story/2021-08-11/l-a-moves-toward-vaccine-requirement-for-restaurants-stores-gyms

August 11, 2021, LA City Council motion to ban the unvaccinated from all public spaces.

https://www.businessinsider.com/china-social-credit-system-punishments-and-rewards-explained-2018-4

Business Insider explains the social credit system of the CCP.

MEN AND WORK

https://www.psychologytoday.com/us/blog/culture-conscious/202104/why-do-men-have-the-most-dangerous-jobs

Lawrence White, Ph.D. suggests that societies where men perform the most dangerous work survive because they protect women.

https://www.bls.gov/news.release/pdf/cfoi.pdf

US Bureau of Labor Statistics 2020 report reveals the most dangerous jobs in the US are performed by men.

https://www.forbes.com/sites/adigaskell/2020/01/09/unemployment-is-prompting-men-to-consider-traditionally-female-jobs/?sh=2a61995473be

Men are moving away from traditionally male (manual labor) jobs to traditionally female jobs.

Made in the USA
Thornton, CO
14 Jan 2022

7192e238-bd51-41a8-8e32-609828d3483aR01